WALDEN REVISITED

WALDEN REVISITED

*A Centennial Tribute to
Henry David Thoreau*

By

George F. Whicher

HENDRICKS HOUSE
New York

Contents

Preface

On the fourth of July, 1845, Henry Thoreau celebrated his independence by moving into the cabin he had built for himself on the shore of Walden Pond. Primarily the move was a practical one. Thoreau at twenty-eight was resolved to be a writer, if possible a poet, and his first move was designed to secure an ample opportunity to commit his thoughts to paper with the least possible sacrifice of precious time.

But more than that, Thoreau at Walden has come to symbolize the plain man unhampered by allegiance to any institution or creed, passing an honest judgment on the ways of society. He represents the ultimate step in the long struggle for freedom from any superimposed authority, the realization of the New World dream of human nature fulfilling itself in accordance with its own inner laws. In him the dignity of the individual is complete. Nothing could be more opposite to the totalitarian doctrines of our times than the transcendentalist's belief in the dignity of man and the supremacy of individual conscience over a debased collective authority.

The essence of the American response to life is embodied in the thought of this unconvinced tester of the supposed advantages of civilization, who loved the wildness of woods and streams and its equivalent in the heart of man. Bronson Alcott called him the most indigenous of American writers.

1

Walden Revisited

No doubt the townsmen of Concord, Massachusetts, celebrated the anniversary of national independence on July 4, 1845, with the customary effusion of gingerbread, spruce beer, and popular oratory. The cradle of liberty may even have been rocked more violently than usual that year, since it was a time of mounting tension. War was gathering on the southern borders. United States troops under General Zachary Taylor were massed at the Sabine River ready for an advance to the Rio Grande. On that very July 4, though Concord would not hear of it until two weeks later, a convention assembled in the Republic of Texas had voted all but unanimously in favor of annexation to the United States. By May, 1846, President Polk had committed the country to a vigorous expression of the bad neighbor policy, otherwise known as manifest destiny. The famous States, as Ralph Waldo Emerson wrote, were soon to be

"Harrying Mexico
With rifle and with knife!"

Concord, whose westernmost section commonly went by the name of "Texas," could hardly have failed to feel that the air was electric with great events.

Or if the town, like New England in general, disapproved of territorial expansion engineered for the benefit of the slave states, it might still be stirred by the unresolved Oregon boundary dispute with Great Britain. A generation before, the British had seized John Jacob Astor's fur-trading post at the mouth of the Columbia River. Now "Fifty-four forty or fight!" was the popular slogan. Two wars threatening to burst into flame were surely enough to make the patriotic kettle simmer.

Yet the most memorable event of that Independence Day passed uncelebrated and almost unnoted. Henry David Thoreau, a young man just short of twenty-eight, moved from his parents' home in the village to a cabin he had built with his own hands on the shore of Walden Pond, a mile and a half away. There was no special significance attached to his selection of a day for his going; the Fourth of July, viewed in the light of eternity, would serve as well as any day. Young Mr. Thoreau was a friend of Ralph Waldo Emerson's, and had often met in the study of that advanced thinker the little group of serious souls whom the neighbors referred to with a smile as the Transcendental Club. A witty lady supplied a definition of transcendental: it meant, she said, "a little beyond." You could think it a little beyond common sense if you liked. Thoreau had recently contributed poems and articles to the short-lived and esoteric *Dial*. But he was also in his own peculiar way a shrewd and practical man who could tell where blueberries grew thickest and was likely to bring home a good string of fish when he chose to go fishing. He seemed to know instinctively how to find the crops that he was best able to gather.

When young men have something to do, they not uncommonly hunt for a place where they may work without distraction. An attic room or a lonely hut in the woods seems at such times the first necessity of their being. Soon after 1840 Thoreau's journal bears witness to the consuming desire for self-realization that possessed him. "It is a great relief when for a few moments in the day we can retire to our chamber and be completely true to ourselves," he wrote in March, 1841. And by December comes this revealing entry: "I want to go soon and live away by the pond, where I shall hear only the wind whispering among the reeds. It will be success if I shall have left myself behind. But my friends ask what I will do when I get there. Will it not be employment enough to watch the progress of the seasons?"

12

Thoreau was probably thinking at this time of the reedy island in the middle of Flint's or Sandy Pond in the township of Lincoln, where his friend Stearns Wheeler had built a shack to study in. He had lived with Wheeler for possibly as much as six weeks. This taste of unimpeded existence only whetted his appetite for more. He was drawn to solitude by what was deepest in his nature. He could no more tell what it was than a lover can set down in words the reasons for his devotion. There was nothing any more original in Thoreau's going to the woods than there is in a young man's falling in love, but in both cases the participant feels that no one has ever had such an experience before.

At various times Thoreau attempted to explain why he elected to live for two years alone in his cabin by Walden. It was the fulfillment, he said, of a dream of his childhood that he should make the spot a nursery of his spirit. Again he declared that he could not account for his action: "To speak sincerely, I went there because I had got ready to go; I left it for the same reason." Even when writing *Walden* he could not decide what his true motives had been. "My purpose in going to Walden Pond was not to live cheaply nor to live dearly there, but to transact some private business with the fewest obstacles." We know that he had a book to put together and wanted long uninterrupted hours for the task. This would have been a sufficient reason if he had left it at that. But there was more to come:

"I went to the woods because I wished to live deliberately, to front only the essential facts of life, and see if I could not learn what it had to teach, and not, when I came to die, discover that I had not lived. I did not wish to live what was not life, living is so dear; nor did I wish to practice resignation, unless it was quite necessary. I wanted to live deep and suck out all the marrow of life, to live so sturdily and Spartan-like as to put to rout all that was not life, to cut a broad swath and shave close, to drive life into a corner, and

13

reduce it to its lowest terms, and, if it proved to be mean, why then to get the whole and genuine meanness of it, and publish its meanness to the world; or if it were sublime, to know it by experience, and be able to give a true account of it in my next excursion."

This ringing statement is no afterthought composed for purposes of publication. It is an expansion of a passage beginning, "I wish to meet the facts of life," written down in Thoreau's journal two days after he had moved into his cabin.

None of these various explanations need be discarded, for all are in some measure true. Yet their variety is significant. Thoreau was usually very conscious of his motives and ready to render an account. But in building a house where he could feel to the uttermost the beauty of solitude he was simply obeying an impulse akin to that which draws the sap upward in spring.

Since he was not aware of a definite motive, some interpretations that have been placed on his retreat to Walden may be ruled out at once. It was not an act of discouragement, nor was there anything sullen in his withdrawal. Thoreau was certainly innocent of any intention to break relations with his family or fellow-townsmen when he left the village. He was not in any serious sense a hermit. The house that he had helped his father to build on the Texas road was still his home, and few days passed that he did not visit it. He saw the friends that he cared to see. Except in his refusal to pay a poll tax to a government whose acts he could not condone, he was not conscious of any falling out between society and himself.

Furthermore, Thoreau was not setting up at Walden a model community of one, with the thought that others might go and do likewise. He did have a message for the discontented and the maladjusted, but it was couched in general terms: "Simplify your life." What form the simplification should take was for each to decide. For Thoreau himself

Walden was conceived in other terms than the Utopian experiments at Brook Farm or Fruitlands. He was not a philanthropic social theorist like George Ripley nor an idealistic reformer like Bronson Alcott. His supreme intention was to mind his own business.

At Walden Pond Thoreau kept house for two years and two months. Then on September 6, 1847, he returned to the village as casually as he had left it, to take care of Emerson's house and family while his friend made a voyage to Europe. The fruits of his stay in the woods were two book manuscripts, one which was practically complete, built around his notes on a boating trip that he had taken several years before, and the other, then only beginning to round into shape, based on the journals that he had kept while living in his cabin. These two products of the years 1845 to 1848 were eventually published as *A Week on the Concord and Merrimack Rivers* in 1849, and *Walden; or, Life in the Woods* in 1854. Out of twenty volumes that now constitute the definitive edition of Thoreau's writings only these two were issued in book form before his death.

His second book, *Walden,* is by common consent the finest expression of New England idealism and one of the greatest books of the nineteenth century. It has been called an American *Robinson Crusoe,* because it tells how a man by his own efforts managed to feed, warm, and shelter himself. But this is to belittle it. Thoreau's book is more many-sided than Defoe's. What he chiefly accomplished was to convey better than any other writer the sense of a special American experience. He knew the meaning of contact with unspoiled wildness, and how it seemed to confirm the hope of a world that was all to be begun anew. Thoreau embodied in the symbol of an independent forest-dweller the American dream of an open frontier and of unlimited expansion. *Walden* like Whitman's *Leaves of Grass* brings to imaginative fulfillment the

15

New World promise of dignity to the individual man. It marks a culmination of the faith implicit in the Declaration of Independence.

A war and a book, both products of American expansiveness, were in the making on the day when Texas voted to join the Union and Henry Thoreau went to live among the pines. Before reading the book it is worth while to consider what kind of man made it, for though Thoreau believed that he had put the best of himself into his books, he committed to life much that he never had opportunity to commit to paper.

2

Biography

Thoreau's life is full of apparent contradictions. It is paradoxical, to begin with, that he, a quintessential New Englander and the only writer native to Concord among those who came to be associated with the town, should be the grandson of a French-speaking immigrant from the Isle of Jersey and should himself have retained slight traces of a French accent. Moreover his father's mother and his mother's father were both of Scottish ancestry. Only through his maternal grandmother, a daughter of the Tory Colonel Elisha Jones of Weston, could Thoreau claim descent from a family long established in Massachusetts. It was in the house of this grandmother on the Virginia Road east of the village that he was born on July 12, 1817.

The following year the Thoreaus moved away from Concord, first to near by Chelmsford, then to Boston. Consequently Henry did not grow up to take his native town for granted, but discovered it with the eager curiosity of a six-year-old when his parents reestablished a home there. John Thoreau, the father, a not quite successful storekeeper, was a reasonably ingenious mechanic and made a comfortable living by the manufacture of lead-pencils, a home industry in which all the family helped. His lively and voluble wife, born Cynthia Dunbar, was not unwilling to take boarders to increase the family income. There were four children, Helen, John, David Henry (as he was christened), and Sophia. Mrs. Thoreau with her younger daughter lived to make a home for Henry until the time of his death.

Northward from Concord lay a great tract of little settled country, full of ponds and streams, where wild creatures were still abundant. The beaver had been hunted out, but muskrat and mink were often seen. Old trappers still recalled anecdotes of wolves and bears. Henry Thoreau and his brother John lived a free outdoor existence, ranging the woods and clearings for nuts and berries and becoming expert with rod and gun. Later in life Henry never hunted bird or beast, and seldom fished, but he was always ready to entertain children with endless stories of his boyish sallies into the wilds. "We seem but to linger in manhood to tell the dreams of our childhood, and they vanish out of memory ere we learn the language," he confided to his journal. Memories of his early days remained vivid to Thoreau all his life.

His parents were respecters of education and ready to deny themselves in order that their children might have it. With some difficulty they managed to acquire a piano for the two girls, who proved to have some musical talent. Henry turned out to be a studious boy, fond of reading, and so when he had finished Concord Academy the family scrimped and saved to send him to Harvard College, where he held a scholarship and contributed what he could earn occasionally by teaching school. In college he spent much time in the library, especially in the alcove where English authors were kept. Though he became reasonably conversant with Latin and Greek classics and remarkably well read in English poetry, his standing in his class was no more than moderately high. Already he was showing a strong preference for going his own way rather than following in the path marked out for him. During his college years Thoreau read Wordsworth, Coleridge, and Carlyle with enthusiastic approval, and he bought and presumably read the little book called *Nature,* Emerson's first publication, which was a kind of manifesto of transcendentalism. But not until he returned to Concord to live was Thoreau really drawn into the current of new thought that was flowing so strongly there.

He graduated from Harvard with the class of 1837. As yet he had discovered no affinity for any particular profession. The great resource for the uncommitted, then as now, was schoolteaching, but an experience of a few days in the common school at Concord convinced Thoreau that he could not succeed as a teacher if he were obliged to use the rod as convention then demanded. Accordingly he joined with his brother John in opening a private school, where discipline was enforced without whipping and where teachers and pupils often took long walks together to study the plant and animal life of the countryside. The routine pursuits of an academy were not neglected. Henry, as the more learned brother, taught Greek, Latin, French, and higher mathematics when it was called for, while John acted as principal, business manager, and teacher of elementary mathematics and English studies. The school, notwithstanding its unusual methods, was a decided success. It flourished for the short time until John's uncertain health obliged the brothers to discontinue it.

Meanwhile Henry had begun to keep a journal and was secretly writing verses. He took a great interest in the village lyceum and regularly lectured before it. His vocation as a writer was declaring itself. One literary man Concord already possessed in Emerson, a tall clergyman-scholar in his middle thirties, who in the year Thoreau graduated from college had electrified Harvard by his address to the Phi Beta Kappa society. As yet Emerson had published little, but he was clearly marked as an intellectual leader. Orthodox people were even beginning to suspect that he might prove a dangerous heretic. Some sentences that Thoreau had written came to the attention of Emerson's sister-in-law, who was boarding at the Thoreaus', and soon the two men were taking walks together and exchanging thoughts. Both secretly longed for perfect companionship; in practice neither could pass the barrier of an ingrained reserve.

Yet even their unconsummated friendship was immensely stimulating. It was Emerson more than anyone else who confirmed and brought to the surface Thoreau's innate powers.

Through Emerson the younger man became a "transcendental brother." He had previously known as his college tutor in Greek the eccentric poet and essayist Jones Very, and during one of his vacation intervals of teaching country school he had met the dynamic Orestes W. Brownson, with whom he had read a little Goethe in the original. But these were uncertain guides. Emerson more than any thinker of the moment was becoming the prophet of New England idealism and self-sufficiency. Under his encouragement Thoreau read oriental scriptures and found himself as an author. His first outpouring of poems occurred while he was living as an inmate of Emerson's house. But something else happened too. A young man in daily contact with a forceful personality must either turn into a disciple or fight hard to preserve his independent identity. Thoreau fought. To the end he never let his sympathy with Emerson's ideas deflect him from the convictions he had decided on for himself.

One freedom that he jealously guarded, no matter what occupation he was nominally pursuing, was an ample leisure for doing what he wanted to do. A broad margin of time was his only luxury. He did not believe in postponing the best of life to some other occasion. He wanted to catch the full savor of experience at once. So he seized the hours that he needed for reading and writing, and saw to it that there was room in the day for rambles afoot or excursions on the placid Musketaquid or Concord River. Now and then he was able to go farther afield. With his brother he had even planned to set up a school in Kentucky, and when this project fell through he made his first visit to Maine in an unsuccessful search for a position as schoolteacher there. It was partly an accident that he remained so closely bound to his native village. He enjoyed the trips he was able to make to distant mountains and waters, and his journal records of such excursions often served him as material for essays or as frames upon which he constructed his books.

20

Early in 1842 Thoreau suffered the sudden and agonizing loss of his brother John, who died of lockjaw. He and Henry had been inseparable companions. They were both attracted by a sensible, merry-hearted girl of seventeen named Ellen Sewall, whose brother Edmund had been a favorite pupil in the Thoreaus' school; and each without knowing what the other was doing proposed marriage to her. Though she liked Henry very much, she refused both offers because of her father's opposition. Later she married happily an undistinguished clergyman. Years afterward Thoreau told Ellen's aunt that he was thinking of Edmund Sewall, his brother John, and Ellen when he wrote of "a hound, a bay horse, and a turtle dove" that he had lost and was forever seeking.

Thoreau never married. His emotional need of a home was satisfied by his attachment to his parents and sisters. It is doubtful if he ever cared for anyone with as deep a devotion as he felt for his brother. For years he could not speak of John's death without tears. Within a few weeks of his own bereavement he was again afflicted when Emerson's entrancing child Waldo died at the age of six. Companionship in grief drew the two friends together more closely than at any other time in their lives.

At Emerson's insistence a quarterly review named by Bronson Alcott the *Dial* was launched late in the year 1840, in the hope that the thinking and writing of the transcendentalists might reach a larger public. The effort was greeted with some amusement. It is doubtful if the *Dial* ever had more than a few hundred readers, but even this limited audience called out the best talents among Emerson's friends. Thoreau, who was living in Emerson's house and attending to Emerson's garden and woodpile, contributed a poem and an essay on the Roman poet Aulus Persius Flaccus to the first number of the new publication. While the *Dial* lasted he continued to offer poems from his now considerable stock and to prepare prose papers on a variety of subjects from notes on the ethical books of the Orient to the "Natural History of Massachusetts." Though Margaret Fuller, who remained the magazine's somewhat captious editor for two years, did not always accept the material Thoreau submitted, she never declined his work without giving ample reasons for her refusal and stimulating suggestions for improvement. Under discipline Thoreau's work did improve. Along with translations and much hack writing that he did for the *Dial* appeared one of his best country essays, "A Winter Walk."

Except for contributing to the *Dial* and to a very few other publications Thoreau was showing little interest in the ordinary occupations of men. At home he helped his father grind graphite for superior crayons, at Emerson's he acted as general handy man, and for the community at large he occasionally accepted a job as a surveyor. On his small earnings he was contented to lead a life of Spartan simplicity, provided he might be unhindered in his favorite pursuits. Like Longfellow, Lowell, and others he was trying to find out how an author could make a living in a country where there was no recognized way of following a literary career. His ultimate solution was highly original in that it involved no compromise of his ideals. But before he came to that he tried teaching once more, spending most of 1843 at Staten Island as a tutor to the children of William Emerson, Ralph Waldo's uninspiring elder brother. There he first saw the ocean, which he was later to know better from Cape Cod. In New York he made the acquaintance of Horace Greeley, founder of the *Tribune*, who had a partiality for radicals and who remained Thoreau's loyal and serviceable friend.

With Greeley's expert help Thoreau was able to place two or three articles in such periodicals as the *Democratic Review* and *Graham's Magazine*, and even to wring payment for his work from reluctant editors. But when the *Dial* ceased publication at the end of its fourth year, he was deprived of the principal medium that brought his writings before the public. Perhaps it was just as well that his energies were not dissipated in minor enterprises. Thrown back upon himself, he did not try to earn his living by his pen—an almost hopeless endeavor, as Edgar Poe was currently proving—but settled the problem of his livelihood by removing to Walden Pond, where he could live on almost nothing and write such books as pleased his fancy. The best years of authorship for him were those that followed.

After a second residence in Emerson's house Thoreau lived for the last thirteen years of his life with his family in a sprawling yellow house not far from the center of Concord. The year that he came home, 1849, was that of the stampede to California. In "Life without Principle" he was later to make his protest against the insensate scramble for wealth. The year was marked for him by the death of his elder sister Helen, by the unsuccessful publication of his first book, by the printing of his powerful essay on "Civil Disobedience" under the title "Resistance to Civil Government" in a kind of aftermath to the *Dial* called *Aesthetic Papers* edited by Elizabeth Peabody, and by his first visit to Cape Cod. He was now well into his thirties, and the exquisite freshness of youth, which Thoreau like Wordsworth felt with exceptional keenness, was passing from him. After the Mexican War and the Gold Rush the high hopes that the transcendentalists had cherished of human nature being born again were likewise fading. Only one decade elapsed between Brook Farm and the Fugitive Slave Law!

Through the 1850's Thoreau occasionally interrupted his quiet routine of reading and writing in the mornings and exploring the neighboring countryside in the afternoons to make excursions to Maine or the White Mountains, or in another mood to New York, where he met Walt Whitman and Henry Ward Beecher. These journeys and their relation to his work will be considered later. After *Walden* appeared in 1854 he became known to a wider public, though he completely avoided the perplexities incident to popularity. Nevertheless, young men were moved to seek him out, and with a few of his admirers he formed warm and lasting connections. The most striking change in his way of life during this period, however, was due to his increasing concern over the question of slavery. Stirred by the humiliating seizure of alleged fugitive slaves in Boston, he delivered a strong address on "Slavery in Massachusetts" before an Anti-Slavery convention at Framingham in 1854. Twice John Brown of Kansas fame came to Concord, and Thoreau was captivated from the start by his simple, uncompromising fervor. After the raid on Harper's Ferry Thoreau was sickened by the pusillanimous tone of the northern press and immediately came out with a flaming defense of Brown's character. Anyone who may be inclined to take seriously Stevenson's too hasty charge that Thoreau was a "skulker" from the normal obligations of society should recall that he was probably the first man in the United States to speak an unhesitating word in favor of a conscientious assailant of the national crime of slavery.

His outburst over John Brown was the last important concentration of Thoreau's powers. Through 1860 and 1861 he was slowly dying of tuberculosis. The Civil War saddened and depressed him. He resented the fact that he was obliged to hear about it. Too late he realized that he would not be able to use a tithe of the enormous accumulation of material gathered in his journal and in his notebooks devoted to Indian lore. As long as he could hold a pen he labored grimly to prepare for the press the five papers that were printed in the *Atlantic Monthly* shortly after his death. In his final revision he cut away every hint of levity such as had once delighted him. With stoical fortitude he bore his wasting illness, trusting in the universal frame of things, and died peacefully on May 6, 1862. His friend Ellery Channing, leaning over to catch his last mutterings, thought he distinguished the words "moose" and "Indian."

In a deeply felt eulogy of his dead friend Emerson said: "His soul was made for the noblest society; he had in a short life exhausted the capabilities of the world; wherever there is knowledge, wherever there is virtue, wherever there is beauty, he will find a home." The truth at the core of this tribute has been proved by the steady growth of Thoreau's reputation.

3

Journeys

Few writers have ever studied the countryside about them with more devoted interest than Thoreau lavished on the woods, meadows, and streams around Concord. During most of his mature life he made it his business to spend some part of every day in a tour of observation by field or river in order that he might note the progress of the seasons in the minutest detail. Often he was abroad at all hours of the night. The many volumes of his journal are an assiduous record of the work of sun, rain, wind, frost, and flowing water, the state of vegetation, the habits of muskrats, frogs, toads, turtles, and fishes, the migration, songs, and nesting of birds. Thoreau was not systematically classifying these things as a scientist might do; he was engaged in deeply absorbing them for the sake of the pleasure that such intimacy with the ways of nature brought him. Bronson Alcott declared that Thoreau was destined to write the perfect "Atlas of Concord." There can be no doubt that he assembled voluminous materials.

Yet for a person so firmly attached to a single spot Thoreau managed to make a fairly large number of excursions to distant points. Two circumstances, moreover, are notable about these travels. He seldom made them because he had business to transact, but purely for the sake of recreation; and though he was a confirmed lover of solitude, he almost always took one companion with him.

Exception to the first of these rules must be made for his journey to New York with his father in 1836 for the purpose of promoting the sale of lead-pencils; for his visit to Maine two years later in search of a school to teach; for his long sojourn on Staten Island while he acted as tutor in the family of William Emerson; for his hurried trip to Fire Island in July, 1850, in the hope of finding relics of Margaret Fuller after her death by shipwreck; and for his third journey to New York and its environs in 1856 when he had the excuse of surveying Marcus Spring's estate at Perth Amboy. Thoreau seldom went to cities unless he had an errand that obliged him to go there, and he commonly left the crowded streets as soon as possible. "I am afraid to travel much or to famous places," he wrote, "lest it might completely dissipate the mind." The only time when he deliberately went sight-seeing was when he and Ellery Channing took a brief excursion by train to Montreal and Quebec in the early autumn of 1850.

But wild places he visited for the joy of the experience. There was no danger that nature would exhaust him. No precise record of all his travels can be recovered from his letters and journals, but by 1852 he could say that he had camped out all night on the tops of four mountains,—Wachusett, Saddleback [Greylock], Katahdin, and Monadnock,—and had rambled over the summits at midnight by moonlight. To the first and last mountains he frequently returned, sometimes merely to climb them in the course of a day's outing, sometimes to camp out for several nights with such companions as Ellery Channing, Harrison Blake, or Edward Hoar. With Channing he made a pedestrian tour in 1844 over the Hoosacs and the Catskills. He first visited the White Mountains and climbed Mount Washington, which he preferred to call by its Indian name of Agiocochook, with his brother John in 1839 as an extension of their boating trip on the Concord and the Merrimack, and he ascended Mount Washington a second time in 1858 with Edward Hoar and others, spending several days perforce at the foot of Tuckerman's Ravine as a consequence of spraining his ankle. His last camping out trip was taken with Channing in 1860, when the two friends passed five nights in a brush shelter on the shoulder of Monadnock.

Thoreau visited Cape Cod four times in all, in 1849, 1850, 1855, and 1857, twice with Channing for company. From the beaches of Staten Island he had gained some first impressions of the ocean, or at least of the lower bay of New York, but on Cape Cod he came as close as he was ever to come to feeling a sense of how the ocean might dominate the lives of those who lived beside it and who looked to it for a living. His was the view of an outsider. He was always emphatically a landsman, more at home on inland rivers than at sea.

The most extensive and on many accounts the most rewarding of his excursions were undertaken partly to observe the methods of river travel in the wilderness of Maine. At the end of his second summer at Walden Pond, on the last day of August, 1846, he journeyed to Bangor and accompanied by a Thatcher cousin who had some connection with the lumber business he penetrated the forest to Mount Katahdin. Only half a dozen ascents of this mountain had then been recorded. Thoreau on this occasion had his first experiences of the untouched wilds. In 1853 he returned to follow the inland waterways of Maine in a birch canoe and see how the moose was hunted. He was again accompanied by his cousin, this time with an Indian hunter as guide. Thoreau's third trip, in July, 1857, took him into the still wilder region of the Allegash and the East Branch of the Penobscot, and brought him into contact with a remarkable personality, the Indian Joe Polis, from whom he learned much of the elemental wisdom of a people long adapted to life in the forest. This taste of the wilderness was the last that deeply affected him. He was to see something of Plains Indians during his journey to Minnesota in 1861, but by that time Thoreau had no energy to absorb what he was seeing. His intention to write a book on the Indians was never carried beyond the preliminary stage of amassing a quantity of notes from the narratives of explorers and fur-traders.

Out of the more than two million words that Thoreau wrote in his journal between 1837 and 1861, the most readily detachable sections were those that had to do with his travels, and it is out of these that all the books that he had time to prepare for the press were made, with the single exception of *Walden*. And even that may be considered in some sense a travel book if one takes literally Thoreau's remark that he had traveled much in Concord. All of his works were the unforced emanations of episodes that he had lived through before he wrote them down.

Yet the best of Thoreau does not lie in mere descriptions of scenery and incidents of travel. His journeys in fact supplied only the framework on which he wove poetic tapestries of reflection and allusion. It is worth while to study briefly the ways in which he secured the kind of heightened effect that distinguishes the work of a master artist in prose from the uncomplicated style of plain communication, which is his basic medium. "In writing," Thoreau said, "conversation should be folded many times thick." The folding in some of his books was quite literal, so that it is possible to distinguish several of the layers.

Probably the thinnest of the narratives of travel is *A Yankee in Canada,* the record of a tour which touched little that deeply concerned Thoreau. He was not at home in French Canada. Neither the grace of its Old World Catholic tradition, as felt in Willa Cather's *Shadows on the Rock,* nor memories of the great historical drama once enacted at Quebec, memories so lively to Francis Parkman, moved him. He gazed at the Plains of Abraham with lack-lustre eye, and passed somewhat carping remarks about the primitive shiftlessness of sawing logs by hand when water-power from the Falls of Montmorenci might be made available. The only overtones awakened by what he observed were overtones of prejudice. Thus at the sight of redcoats in the citadel of Quebec all his dislike of regimentation comes to the surface, and he applies caustic reflections to the scene he is describing, as for example: "It is impossible to give the soldier a good education without making him a deserter." This may be a profound observation in its way, but making it just at this point

29

is like propounding a critical comment on the textile industry at the moment when the flag is being raised.

When Thoreau is truly at ease and happy in his material, the incongruous superposition of thought upon fact yields at once to more subtle implications. The tensions of emotional involvement multiply the interfoldings of awareness. So in the following sentence from "A Walk to Wachusett" the primary factual perception of the degree of light within the tent is overlaid first by a sense of the immensities of space in the night outside, then by a whimsical feeling of fellowship with the heavenly bodies, and finally by a realization of their infiniteness and mystery: "It was at no time darker than twilight within the tent, and we could easily see the moon through its transparent roof as we lay; for there was the moon still above us, with Jupiter and Saturn on either hand, looking down on Wachusett, and it was a satisfaction to know that they were our fellow-travelers still, as high and out of reach as our own destiny."

Or consider, overleaf in the same essay, a description of sunrise where the actual scene is sublimated by imperceptible stages into a poetic comparison: "At length we saw the sun rise up out of the sea, and shine on Massachusetts; and from this moment the atmosphere grew more and more transparent till the time of our departure, and we began to realize the extent of our view, and how the earth, in some degree, answered to the heavens in breadth, the white villages to the constellations in the sky."

These passages are good examples of Thoreau's almost magical power to convey in words the effect of space and cold pure air and the light of dawn. He found the perfect word for his style when he spoke of it as "hypaethral," borrowing a word that is applied to a type of Egyptian temple open to the sun and air.

He can also be of the earth earthy and write with undiminished gusto. In the three papers that make up his book on

e based. Emerson found it next to impossible to
rkling single sentences into coherent wholes, and
endentalists when they wrote books were driven
dry mechanical devices to secure an appearance
composition which not infrequently failed to sus-
eful notion that whatever is sincerely spoken by
arate person will be found to have a sufficient
tency. In theory the ideal book should unfold
s naturally as leaves in the spring. In practice
nscendental writer produced was often a miscel-
ch a semblance of form was imposed as by after-

of obtaining an artificial beginning and end was
book around the record of a journey or excur-
ough the "middle" which Aristotle also held to
should turn out to be little else than a mere un-
continuum. This device, as has already been
eau frequently employed. Another kind of me-
n might be secured by limiting the work to a
f time, such as a day, a week, a season, or a year.
ct Thoreau was anticipated by Margaret Fuller,
iece of original writing was the narrative of a
e unsettled frontier country of Illinois and Wis-
the title *Summer on the Lakes*. Since the au-
this work has always been reprinted in an edited
h reduces it to three-fifths of its former length
t a simple description of travel. As Margaret
osed it, however, the book was a characteristic
al miscellany which deserves examination for its
ence on Thoreau's practice.
r had no idea of limiting her material to exter-
ons of the country she was to pass through. Her
ence invites the reader to share "such foot-notes
de on the pages of my life during this summer's
The book, in other words, was to be a record

The Maine Woods he was recording impressions of the wild, half brutal world of the backwoods, where the savage upthrust of the forest was only varied by the reckless slashings of lumbermen and the wanton killings of moose and deer by hide-hunters. Plenty of rawness and ugliness is in the book, the squalor of the roving natives, the putrifying carcasses of moose lying in the shallows where they have been slaughtered and skinned. But in the midst of his faithful and often prosaic recording of these things there are moments when the spirit of the wilderness is marvelously rendered. The following passage has been often quoted: "Once, when Joe had called again, and we were listening for moose, we heard, come faintly echoing, or creeping from far through the moss-clad aisles, a dull, dry rushing sound with a solid core to it, yet as if half smothered under the grasp of the luxuriant and fungus-like forest, like the shutting of a door in some distant entry of the damp and shaggy wilderness. If we had not been there, no mortal had heard it. When we asked Joe in a whisper what it was, he answered, 'Tree fall'."

The fact that Thoreau returned at intervals to the Maine woods gives his account of these excursions a cumulative force which is missing from the slender narrative of his Canadian tour. Each time he comes back he seems to be penetrating further into the mystery of the forest, and to go on from where he left off before. The "Ktaadn" chapter gives a general first impression of the forest itself as a phenomenon, the "Chesuncook" excursion is concerned mainly with how lumbermen and hunters live and travel on the lakes and rivers of the interior, and finally in the paper on "The Allegash and East Branch" Thoreau is exploring not so much the country as the mind of the Indian. The superposing of each successive chapter upon the insights that have gone before gives the book as a whole a power of density and depth that is impressive.

Cape Cod like the Maine woods was strange country to a

resident of an inland town. In writing of it Thoreau again had the advantage of several sets of observations or field notes made at different times. When he composed a book out of his journal entries, he adopted a device more elaborate and more successful than that of printing in succession the narratives of his various trips. Taking his first pedestrian tour as a basis, he imposed upon it materials subsequently gathered, thus fusing all that he had to say into one unified and enriched narrative. A happy consequence of this method, which Thoreau was to use again when he compressed the story of his two years at Walden within the compass of a single year, was the multiplication of encounters with people of the region and other incidents of travel. In any one trip such meetings would be infrequent and hence vividly remembered. In combination none of the vividness is lost, while the intervals of sheer factual description are shortened. By such interfolding the whole book is enlivened. It is no accident that readers have found *Cape Cod* the most human of Thoreau's travel books.

In none of these works, however, does Thoreau's writing reach the level of sustained power that marks his *Week* and *Walden.* Something more went into the making of these two projections of a soul in matter than mere honesty of recording, or deftness in expression, or skill in the combining of factual impressions. Still the basis on which Thoreau worked was invariably a solid foundation of fact drawn from his journals.

Thoreau would hardly
wrote it," as Mrs. Stowe
say of *Uncle Tom's Cab*
ists was suspicious of boo
More than the surface of
thought, in the creation
should rise from the dep
tated by a more than hur
ible outpouring like the f
have organic growth like
put it, "the work we choo

This theory of literary
clearness in Thoreau's po
written out of a man's "
prove "weak and shallow
erly it may be contrived.

"But if with bended
Listening behind n
With faith superior to
More anxious to ke

"Making my soul acco
Unto the flame my
Then will the verse fo
Time cannot bend

By some such process of
deed be produced a strikin
line. It may even suffice fo
brief lyric cry. But sheer
principle of construction o

works can
weld his sp
other trans
to adopt s
of unity in
tain the ho
a simple s
inner con
into form
what the
lany on w
thought.

One w
to build t
sion, even
be necessa
differentia
noted, T
chanical
single un
In this re
whose fir
journey t
consin u
thor's de
version
and mal
Fuller c
transcen
possible
Miss
nal obse
opening
as may
wanderi

of random thoughts as well as sights, and anything that occupied the author's mind might be considered germane to her subject. So among verbal pictures of Niagara, Mackinaw, and the prairies, and pertinent remarks on the Indians and the life of the white settlers, are mingled poems composed during the trip, a tale of Mariana which is not improbably a bit of disguised autobiography, reflections on books read, a long digression on a German girl who possessed visionary powers, and other extraneous material. Miss Fuller even manages to insert a glowing appreciation of Titian's painting of Venus and Adonis "with no excuse, except that it came to memory at the time." The saying that all is grist that comes to the mill has seldom been given more uninhibited application.

Written by a member of Thoreau's intimate circle and published a year before he went to Walden and five years before his own first book, *Summer on the Lakes* must have been a kind of model for him to excel when he meditated on the writing of the *Week*. Both books are ostensibly records of travel, but records enriched by occasional verses, philosophical and moral reflections, essays, and digressions of all kinds. Each takes as its ultimate object the entertainment of the reader by a great variety of substance, which will also prove instructive and will in a way not too clearly defined indicate the scope of man's powers and the interactions of man and nature.

In 1839 John and Henry Thoreau, young schoolteachers in their early twenties, launched on the placid Concord River a boat that they had built themselves and named the Musketaquid. It was large enough so that both could row at once and was rigged with two small masts and sails. In this craft they loaded provisions, buffalo robes, and a home-made tent, and on the last day of August pushed off for a thirteen-day adventure, partly afloat and partly ashore, from Concord to the summit of Mount Washington. The expanded journal of the fluvial portion of this excursion, the first of Henry's longer camping trips, made up approximately one half of the book that he put together during the first year that he lived at Walden.

The first step in preparing the manuscript for publication was the decision to omit entirely the half of the diary that had to do with land travel and mountain climbing. This aspect of the trip is summarized in a few pages. There remained the cycle of one week, Saturday to Friday, and Thoreau took his luck as he found it and wrote one chapter around each day with a slight prologue to introduce the whole. It was part of his theory not to disturb the setting of his thoughts any more than he could help. Better print them in journal form as they actually occurred than try to detach and rearrange them in coherent essays. If his thoughts had been golden, he would have wanted to present to his readers not the refined metal, nor even chance nuggets, but the whole mine.

Next, as a beginning of the process of elaboration or enrichment, Thoreau did what Herman Melville and other travel writers have commonly done: he read widely in town histories, colonial chronicles, and such descriptive books as were available and collected a mass of anecdotes, adventures, statistics, and picturesque factual material that might be worked into his record from point to point. Thus in connection with the scenes he was reviewing he was led naturally to recall the old frontier ballad of "Lovewell's Fight" and to retell the story of Hannah Dustin's exploit in escaping from the Indians that had taken her captive. A great deal of such local detail, culled from various records, is given incidentally as he goes along.

But besides supplementing the journal of his travels from local history, Thoreau like Margaret Fuller inserted in the book pieces of verse and prose that were little or not at all connected with the rowers' progress on the rivers, except that like the essay chapters in Melville's *Moby Dick* these digressions serve to give the reader a sense of the passage of time and of distance covered without the necessity of watching every operation that carries the vessel onward. In thus alternating selections from his commonplace book with pages from his diary Thoreau was not merely inventing a device to secure variety, as Mark Twain, for example, did when he interjected "Jim Baker's Blue-Jay Yarn" in the midst of a description of student life at the University of Heidelberg. He was attempting to create a new species of travel book, one that would parallel the physical journey of a young man on the waters with the procession of a soul on the stream of time. Hence he drew largely on work that he had already published as well as on new pages from his notebooks. Readers should have him in the lump. From the *Dial* came essays on Aulus Persius Flaccus and on Anacreon, and a number of the more than fifty poems or scraps of poems that he scattered through the text. Besides a discussion of fishes which rose naturally from a consideration of the watery road on which the voyagers were proceeding and from the sight of a fisherman on the bank, Thoreau took advantage of the coming of Sunday to air his views on mythology and religion, Greek, Hindoo, and Christian. But with no shadow of excuse he introduced in his Sunday chapter also an essay on Books and Reading, and in the course of Wednesday the famous essay on Friendship, while his discussion of Poetry is intermittent and ranges over Homer, Ossian, Chaucer, and Goethe, in addition to the two classical writers previously mentioned. Lowell, who seldom did justice to Thoreau, missed the point when in reviewing the *Week* he spoke of these digressions as "snags" and considered them "out of proportion and out of place." They are essential to the kind of work that Thoreau planned. Without them it would have been impossible for him to achieve that effect of "happy fortuity" as of thoughts bubbling up from a living spring which Lowell rightly praises.

The "hypaethral" quality of Thoreau's writing is very pure in some of the fluvial passages of the *Week* and in descriptions of rambles in the Hoosacs and on Greylock. Only Hazlitt can so describe the lift of spirits that comes of going a journey. But there are many good outdoor books, full of sun and air, that do not impress the reader as so vitally a part of the writer's being as this one. Probably Henry Seidel Canby in his ample biography of Thoreau has come as near as a critic can to explaining the elusive and dynamic power of these pages. "I believe," he writes, "that his deep love for John, the tension which rose between them over Ellen, which must have colored the memory of those intimate days on the rivers, and John's sudden and terrible death, gave to his many tentative records of the voyage a significance and a worth which no casual tramping over the Catskills or on Cape Cod with Ellery could equal." It is possible also to suppose that the freedom of his life at Walden had something to do with the buoyancy and exuberance of his writing and with the extraordinary release of his energies between 1845 and 1848 when both the books that appeared during his lifetime were in effect composed. The *Week* may be in some conventional respects an ungainly book, but it indubitably comes alive as few books of travel ever do.

By the time he left Walden Thoreau had the manuscripts of his two books in hand and was ready to look for a publisher for the first. As the author of a few pieces of prose and verse in the transcendental *Dial* he could hardly have expected that a commercial firm would see much profit in his volume, and in fact none did. After four different publishers had declined to undertake the work at their own risk, Thoreau commissioned the house of James Monroe of Boston and Cambridge, the publishers of Emerson's *Essays* and *Poems,* to bring out the book at his expense. Many hours of surveying and many gross of lead-pencils went to the paying for it. When *A Week on the Concord and Merrimack Riv-*

ers appeared in the summer of 1849, it was reviewed not unkindly by friends such as Lowell and George Ripley, but roused little general interest in that feverish year of the California Gold Rush. In the autumn of 1853 the publishers ("falsely so called," muttered Thoreau) insisted on returning to the author 706 unsold copies out of an edition of one thousand. After stacking up the bundles like cordwood along the wall of his attic bedroom Thoreau entered in his journal the immortal comment: "I have now a library of nearly nine hundred volumes, over seven hundred of which I wrote myself."

No external appreciation was needed to confirm Thoreau's conviction of the soundness of his work, yet it is pleasant to recall that a just appraisal of the book which the public would not buy was put on record even before the manuscript was completed. After hearing some passages from the work in progress read in Thoreau's cabin, Bronson Alcott entered in his journal for March 16, 1847, a verdict which may still stand as definitive:

"The book is purely American, fragrant with the lives of New England woods and streams, and could have been written nowhere else. It preserves to us whatever of the wild and mystic remains to us along our brooksides and rivers, and is written in a style as picturesque and flowing as the streams he sails on . . .

"It has the merit, moreover, that somehow, despite all presumptions to the contrary, the sod and sap and fibre and flavour of New England have found at last a clear relation to the literature of other and classic lands . . . Egypt, India, Greece, England, flow from the poet's hand as he scoops the waters for us from the rivers . . .

"Especially am I touched by this soundness, this aboriginal vigour, as if a man had once more come into Nature . . .

"I came home at midnight through the woody snow-paths and slept with the pleasing dream that presently the press would place on my shelves a second beside· my first volume, also written by my townsman, and give me two books to be proud of: Emerson's *Poems* and Thoreau's *Week*."

5

Reading

Alcott's testimony to Thoreau's familiarity with the litera-
tures of other lands is not to be dismissed as a mere rhetori-
cal flourish. His knowledge was genuinely acquired by hard
reading. Books to him were not, as Emerson intimated they
should be, "for the scholar's idle times," but for hours of
strenuous application. "To read well," wrote Thoreau, "that
is, to read true books in a true spirit, is a noble exercise, and
one that will task the reader more than any exercise which
the customs of the day esteem. It requires a training such as
the athletes underwent, the steady intention almost of the
whole life to this object." His specifications for satisfactory
reading matter are surely such as only a reader of athletic
mind would make. "Books, not which afford us a cowering
enjoyment, but in which each thought is of unusual daring;
such as an idle man cannot read, and a timid one would not
be entertained by, which even make us dangerous to exist-
ing institutions,—such call I good books." On subjects that
concerned him Thoreau read widely, but his preference was
for a few inexhaustible books to which he could return again
and again.

Before he entered Harvard, if we may believe tradition, he
had performed a feat of reading that required no little steady
intention: he had read straight through the twenty-one volumes of Alexander Chalmers' *Works of the English Poets,
from Chaucer to Cowper* (London, 1810). He is said to
have repeated the same exploit at a later date. These comprehensive assaults on the whole realm of English poetry
made him familiar with several early writers that are seldom
opened, such as Gower and Lydgate as well as Chaucer.
They also determined his taste for the late Elizabethan and
early Jacobean authors, such men as Daniel, Drayton, Ra-

leigh, and Donne among Shakespeare's contemporaries, and from the later group the religious poets Herbert, Vaughan, and Crashaw. A special favorite, Quarles, was a later discovery. Thoreau preferred Milton as a poet to Shakespeare. It is noteworthy that his taste was not for poets that the nineteenth century delighted to honor. With the possible exception of Herbert none of the lesser men that he speaks of were greatly admired at the time. In reading as in life Thoreau liked to find his own way about.

He was reasonably acquainted also with the prose writers of the seventeenth century, as may be evident to one who listens for echoes of the English Bible or the rhythms of Sir Thomas Browne in the cadences of Thoreau's sentences. An obviously imitative passage, with a geographical borrowing from *Paradise Lost* to boot, is the last paragraph of the chapter on "The Pond in Winter" in *Walden*.

Next to English writers he early felt the influence of the Greek and Latin classics, in which he was thoroughly drilled both in school and in college. Thoreau was in fact the best linguist of the Concord group. According to his friend and biographer Frank Sanborn, he could read Latin and French as easily as English, was conversant with Greek, and possessed some knowledge of German, Spanish, and Italian. He was not fond of the modern languages, however, and he seems to have read few masterpieces in the original, except in the ancient tongues. His enthusiasm for Greek gradually waned. While he was spending six hours a day, in his early twenties, in the drudgery of schoolteaching, he was as willing to read a few extra pages of Homer as to go for a walk. He made English translations of two Aeschylean plays and of a few poems by Pindar and the pseudo-Anacreon. The *Iliad* was one of the few books that he took to his Walden cabin, but he confessed that he seldom found time to look at it. Thereafter there are few records of his reading further in Greek. Unlike Emerson he was not attracted by Plato.

In Latin, on the other hand, he continued to explore with zest, soon turning away from the generally read masters of prose and verse to less known satirists such as Persius and to writers of utilitarian prose like Columella and Varro. He was as ready as ever to justify his idiosyncrasies. "If the writers of the bronze age are most suggestive to thee, confine thyself to them, and leave those of the Augustan age to dust and to the book worms." Though Thoreau's sense of style was no doubt shaped in some degree by his early immersion in the classics, he was not one to follow tamely the ancient models. Before long he was asserting his own taste in the selection of writers who handled plain factual matters connected with plowland and vineyard, and leaving his Virgil and Horace to teach elegance to those who might value it.

In Thoreau's opinion no poetry, either English or classical, adequately expressed the freshness and vigor that he felt in wild nature. All the literature he knew seemed tame and artificial. Only in momentary flashes in works of the highest genius, in *Hamlet* or the *Iliad,* could he discover passages whose inevitable perfection suggested the expanding of buds at the approach of spring. He was demanding what no civilized culture could achieve, an unconscious flowering of man's being into art. Mythology, the age-old accumulations of folk-wisdom, came nearer than any premeditated poetry to satisfying his yearning for unspoiled primitive naturalness, "wild lands where no settler has squatted." Nothing was more characteristic of him than his quaint way of fusing scraps of Greek myth and legend with the New England countryside, as when in *Walden* he sees the weeds in his beanfield as "Trojans who had sun and rain and dews on their side," or as when he revives the obscure tradition that Hebe, the cupbearer of Jove and the personfication of immortal youth, was the "daughter of Juno and wild lettuce." One can hear the Yankee twang as he adds: "She was probably the only thoroughly sound-conditioned, healthy, and robust young lady that ever walked the globe, and wherever she came it was spring."

It was typical of a mind early stored with classical images that the hum of telegraph wires should seem to speak of Greece and the Muses. Let us grant that in Thoreau's youthful writing the frequent resort to classical allusion seems often far-fetched and pedantic. It is difficult to believe that Achilles and Hector have left footprints on the Concord meadows. Yet the same miracle of imaginative acclimatization that made the Athenian Theseus a duke and citizen of Shakespeare's London can at moments almost persuade us that Homer's trumpets still sound along the Musketaquid. Consider the poetic fusion of the disparate elements in the following passage: "Morning brings back the heroic ages. I was as much affected by the faint hum of a mosquito making its invisible and unimaginable tour through my apartment at earliest dawn, when I was sitting with door and windows open, as I could be by any trumpet that ever sang of fame. It was Homer's requiem; itself an Iliad and Odyssey in the air, singing its own wrath and wanderings." What two words can more fittingly convey the thin, angry whine of the mosquito's air-borne assault than the two key-words of Homer's epics, Achilles' *wrath,* Odysseus' *wanderings?* Only a fancy akin to Donne's, however, could detect and successfully exploit such remote analogies, and only a master of tonal effects could so concentrate nasal consonants as to make the words faintly vibrant with an echo of the mosquito's hum.

A desire to deepen his mystical love of nature was probably what led Thoreau to explore the scriptures of India, China, and Persia, the third great reservoir from which he drew inspiration for his work. Emerson likewise was a devotee of oriental writings, and it was in Emerson's study that Thoreau first soaked himself in the books of the East. This was in the year 1841, when at the age of twenty-four Thoreau seems first to have made up his mind to devote himself to a literary career. Previous to this he must have known the paraphrases of oriental poems by Sir William Jones and the comprehensive essay "On the Poetry of the Eastern Nations" contained in Chalmers' *Poets*. He was not entirely a novice in respect to the great books of Asia when he set himself to examine them more closely and to make excerpts for several articles that appeared in the *Dial* in 1843 and 1844. Vigorous entries in his journal attest his first ardent enthusiasm for Manu, Confucius, Zoroaster, and the like, and reveal the deeper insight into these writings that came to him after he had spent years in their company. When in 1855 a British visitor named Thomas Cholmondeley wished to give Thoreau what would please him most, he sent from London a "nest of Indian books" consisting of forty-four volumes of Hindoo scriptures, some in English, French, or Latin translation, others in the original Sanskrit. By that time the oriental classics were familiar friends to Emerson, Alcott, and Thoreau. From them they drew telling sayings in support of the ideas that were already theirs. It should not be supposed that any of the transcendentalists penetrated to the actual meaning and spirit of the wisdom of the East.

The effect of Thoreau's reading of oriental philosophy is superficially evident in the quotations scattered through his works and in the occasional parables modeled on the oriental pattern that occur in *Walden*. How far he accepted some of the religious practices and underlying ideas of Hindoo ascetic philosophy it is not possible to say precisely. During his sojourn at the pond he seems to have experimented with austerities of diet and other ascetic practices, and what he records on one occasion about sitting in his sunny doorway from sunrise till noon, rapt in revery, would lead one to suppose that he was attempting to induce a state of mystical contemplation akin to that sacramentally practiced by oriental devotees of the *yoga*. With the rules of this system of ascetic discipline

45

Thoreau was certainly acquainted, since he wrote to his friend Harrison Blake in 1849: "To some extent, and at rare intervals, even I am a yogi." Such exercises, even amateurishly and unsystematically followed, may have served to deepen Thoreau's sense of the spirituality of life and to carry him above the petty routine of a small New England village.

From Concord Thoreau liked to send his imagination ranging to distant lands and strange seas. He was an avid reader of travel books, including narratives of Elizabethan exploration such as *Purchas His Pilgrimes.* He kept up with recent voyages of discovery also, often noting in his journal some curious bit of information relating to Africa or the Arctic or Australia and the South Seas. Bits of this flotsam and jetsam are strewn through his works. He was not neglectful of American travels either, but showed an acquaintance ranging from Timothy Dwight's account of his trips through New England to Benjamin G. Ferris's *Utah and the Mormons.* Perfect books for Thoreau were Charles Darwin's *Voyage of the Beagle,* which combined descriptions and anecdotes of South America with much scientific lore, and William Bartram's *Travels,* with its accounts of the virgin forests and Indian tribes of the southern United States.

To supplement his own observations of the flora and fauna around Concord Thoreau had browsed through all the natural histories and herbals he could find. He knew Topsell's quaint *History of Four-Footed Beasts,* Gerard's *Herbal,* Evelyn's *Sylva,* and other authorities of the Renaissance and seventeenth century. He refers to John Josselyn's description of *New England's Rarities* and to Gilbert White's *Natural History of Selborne.* More modern scientific books and government reports on animals, birds, reptiles, fishes, insects, and plants were his constant study.

Whenever he visited a place like Cape Cod or Plymouth, he was sure to look up the histories of its discovery and settlement. As connected with the former he had read the voyages of Gilbert, Gosnold, Archer, Brereton, Pring, and Captain John Smith. Of the colonial chronicles of Plymouth he was familiar with Bradford, Winslow, and Mourt's *Relation,* and he had read the journal of Boston's Governor Winthrop. He also consulted such later histories as Edward Johnson's *Wonder-Working Providence* and Cotton Mather's *Magnalia Christi Americana.*

The literature of the early Indian wars and captivities had from the first attracted his attention. Partly from still surviving local traditions and partly from books he had derived the story of Hannah Dustin's famous escape. He knew the vivid narratives of Mrs. Mary Rowlandson and of Joseph Bartlett. Samuel Penhallow was his authority for the Indian wars of Maine, and he enjoyed repeating the stirring ballad of "Lovewell's Fight" which commemorated a bloody episode of the struggle down east.

Much of his detailed information about the New England past was gained from such books as J. W. Barber's *Historical Collections,* or from state and town histories. He mentions at one time or another reading histories of New Hampshire (Jeremy Belknap), Virginia (Robert Beverly), Vermont (Zachary Thompson), and Connecticut (Samuel Peters).

He had scanned extensively the records of the American frontier, beginning with such French sources as Champlain's *Voyages* and the Jesuit *Relations* and continuing with Charlevoix and other historians of New France. Jonathan Carver's *Travels Through the Interior Parts of North America* and Alexander Henry's *Travels and Adventures in Canada* were favorite classics of the fur-trade with many anecdotes of Indians in the western regions. In the later years of his life Thoreau read everything he could find on the American aborigines, as well as studying the red men wherever he could meet them from Maine to Minnesota. His voluminous notes are now in the Pierrepont Morgan Library in New

York. The book that he dreamed of making on the Indian was never written.

In these factual books and records of travel and exploration Thoreau encountered the kind of gritty, unaffected prose that pleased him. Here was the antidote to the effeminacy of his contemporaries. "The sentences written by such rude hands are nervous and tough, like hardened thongs, the sinews of the deer, or the roots of the pine." Here were "sentences which . . . lie like boulders on the page, up and down or across." They supplied him with ballast while his contact with the mystical writings of the orient served as a great wind to fill his sails and to drive him forward in a quest for perfection. It should be remarked that Thoreau, like Herman Melville, felt no opposition between lofty spiritual contemplation and an abundant sensuous delight in the earth. The perfection that he wanted was not to be gained by a denial of what was dear to him in this world. And so his choice of reading reflects his attachment to both realms of being.

6

Friendships

Friends, Thoreau found, are not easily subordinated to a program of perfection. Books, nature, the day's tasks, may all be manipulated to suit the soul's needs, but friends constitute an unpredictable element. It is too much to hope that a friend's arrival will never be untimely, nor his departure welcome. Perhaps a perfectionist can only exist in solitude. In the give and take of human intercourse the illusion of spiritual advancement is difficult to maintain. Consequently in so far as Thoreau became the Yankee counterpart of a *yogi* he was unfitted for friendship. It is significant that his most successful human relations, outside his own family, were established with children, or with farmers, woodchoppers, and village reprobates. In the presence of respectable folks he generally maintained a polite but impenetrable reserve. "I love Henry," said the intellectual Elizabeth Hoar, "but I cannot like him; and as for taking his arm, I should as soon think of taking the arm of an elm-tree." Emerson endorsed, if he did not originate, this remark.

Nevertheless Thoreau gave a great deal of attention to elaborating a theory of friendship and to testing it in practice. His experiments were not as devoid of success as one might suppose from reading the passages in his journal where he bemoans the fact that friends in actuality never come up to expectations. If he was never able to find the ideal friend of his imagination, he was not unwilling to acknowledge the solid satisfactions he derived even from the partial fulfillment of his dream.

Both Emerson and Thoreau published essays on Friendship during the 1840's, Emerson in the first series of his *Essays* (1841) and Thoreau in the *Week* (1849). To place them side by side is to illuminate some important differences between the two men. Each, as might be expected, had no use for the merely utilitarian aspects of friendship, yet Emerson in the midst of his etherealizing of the friendly relationship never lost sight of the principle of self-development. "We must be our own before we can be another's." Friends supply one of the conditions that enable a man to realize his personality. "The soul environs itself with friends that it may enter into a grander self-acquaintance or solitude; and it goes alone for a season that it may exalt its conversation or society." Society and solitude are the systole and diastole of life. But Emerson recoiled from any thought of combining friendship with "politics and chat and neighborly conveniences." These can be had cheaply. "Should not the society of my friend be to me poetic, pure, universal and great as nature itself?" The ideal of friendship "may be said to require natures so rare . . . that its satisfaction can very seldom be assured." "Friends such as we desire are dreams and fables." So difficult is perfect intercourse on the high ground that Emerson takes, that before he has finished he has in effect abolished the conception of friendship and set up instead a solipsistic ideal of benevolent friendliness that never asks to be requited. When indeed did Emerson ever know an intimacy such as he describes? His essay gives the impression of comment by an outsider.

In the case of Thoreau, however, the actuality of the experience is written in his pulse-beats. "The only danger in Friendship is that it will end." He like Emerson is aware of the possibility of disappointment when friends fail to meet on an ideal level. He knows that friendship is evanescent and cannot be long sustained at its best, that its joys must be mainly of expectation and retrospect. But what for Emerson is essentially a form of education is for Thoreau a means of rapture. "There are passages of affection in our intercourse with mortal men and women, such as no prophecy had taught us to expect, which transcend our earthly life, and anticipate Heaven for us." Defects in intimacy he can take in his stride. "Ignorance and bungling with love are better than wisdom and skill without." And though he also realizes that intercourse with friends is improved by intervals of solitude, he conceives of these intervals not as occasions for consolidating one's gains in a grander self-acquaintance but for preparing oneself for a loftier intimacy. His tone is poetic. "Silence is the ambrosial night in the intercourse of Friends, in which their sincerity is recruited and takes deeper root."

There can be little doubt that Thoreau's essay on Friendship is a tribute to his brother John, his only close comrade until the elder brother's sudden and painful death. And mingled with recollections of that dear companionship were ecstatic memories of an idealized relationship with Ellen Sewall, a friend whom he cherished all the more because she remained aloof. Embedded in the essay is a poem that he had written to express his affectionate regard for the boy Edmund Sewall, her brother, on whose potential but unripened friendship Thoreau set a romantically high value. Other poems that spoke of Ellen herself appeared on an earlier page. Indeed he could hardly think of boating on the Concord without recalling the brief and happy visit that she had paid to his family when he and John had taken her rowing. The reference is explicit:

"On this same stream a maiden once sailed in my boat, thus unattended but by invisible guardians, and as she sat in the prow there was nothing but herself between the steersman and the sky. I could then say with the poet,

> "Sweet falls the summer air
> Over her frame who sails with me;
> Her way like that is beautifully free,
>   Her nature far more rare
> And is her constant heart of virgin purity"—

51

"At evening, still the very stars seem but this maiden's emissaries and reporters of her progress.

"Low in the eastern sky
Is set thy glancing eye" . . . .

Thoreau's most noted friend was Emerson himself. Their relationship was at first extremely cordial. The younger man, just out of college, responded to a personal stimulation that was proving extremely attractive to young men everywhere. In Emerson he saw "more of the divine realized" than in any other person. "In his world every man would be a poet, Love would reign, Beauty would take place, Man and Nature would harmonize." Emerson in turn enjoyed the singular experience of discovering a living embodiment of his American Scholar, moulded by nature, books, and action, right in his home town. It should be noted that Emerson's Phi Beta Kappa address was written before he knew Thoreau, and equally that Thoreau had shaped his character independently of Emerson. There could be no question of imitation or discipleship.

But it is not certain that Emerson was able to avoid a few proprietary airs. "My good Henry Thoreau," he wrote in 1838, "made this else solitary afternoon sunny with his simplicity and clear perception." And again in 1841: "I told Henry Thoreau that his freedom is in the form, but he does not disclose new matter. I am very familiar with all his thoughts,—they are my own quite originally drest." Thoreau may have had his own ideas about his originality. If he became aware of the local jests that pictured him as trying to imitate Emerson in gait and gesture, he could hardly have avoided being sensitive on the subject. After James Russell Lowell in *A Fable for Critics* (1848) had associated him with one who was accustomed to

"Tread in Emerson's tracks, with legs painfully short,"

Thoreau cannot have failed to know that he was being ridiculed. The natural effect would have been to make him emphasize in every possible way his divergencies from the man who was popularly regarded as his master.

By 1853 each man was confiding to his journal how difficult he found it to converse with the other. On a day late in May Thoreau wrote: "Talked, or tried to talk, with R.W.E. Lost my time—nay, almost my identity. He, assuming a false opposition where there was no difference of opinion, talked to the wind—told me what I knew—and I lost my time trying to imagine myself somebody else to oppose him."

In the course of the following month Emerson noted that Thoreau was "military" and "rarely sweet." "One would say that, as Webster could never speak without an antagonist, so Henry does not feel himself except in opposition. He wants a fallacy to expose, a blunder to pillory, requires a little sense of victory, a roll of the drums, to call his powers into full exercise."

Thoreau was fully conscious that he was parting company with the most sympathetic friend he ever had. Each was pursuing his proper path. The nature of the divergence was perhaps not as clear then as it has since become. The early years of their acquaintance had coincided with the peak of the transcendental excitement, when Emerson was sounding the call for a new relation of man to the universe and pleading with Americans to discover the divine nature inherent in their being. But, as Thoreau wrote in one of his letters, the whole enterprise of the nation was "not an upward, but a westward one, toward Oregon, California, Japan, etc." The message of the transcendental prophet was unheeded, and he remained an increasingly lonely figure on his mount of vision. Thoreau and Emerson differed profoundly in the way each proceeded from that point. Emerson tended to recede more and more into a mild and mystical meliorism which held that nature would inevitably right what was wrong and bring all back to an even keel. Thoreau, on the contrary, though seemingly in retreat from men to muskrats, moved in the direction of civil disobedience. If the state was dull and evil, it was for men of conscience to do something about it. At the time of the John Brown incident Thoreau could not have been mistaken as a follower of Emerson.

Bronson Alcott, as early as 1852, became aware of the difference in the quality of his two friends. We find him writing in his journal for January 6: "Emerson said fine things last night about 'Wealth,' but there are finer things far to be said in praise of Poverty, which it takes a person superior to Emerson even to say worthily. Thoreau is the better man, perhaps, to celebrate that estate, about which he knows much, and which he wears as an ornament about himself. . . . Eloquent, wise, and witty as were the orator's praises of Gold, and just to this transition period of civilization, the merchant's day as none ever before—still the moral laws were too faintly implied, and so left not without detriment in the auditor's mind." Alcott was correct in discerning a Cromwellian fiber in the younger man.

With the high-minded and intransigent Alcott himself Thoreau remained in close accord. Though the Connecticut idealist was three years older than Emerson, he seemed to Thoreau at thirty "the youngest man of his age we have seen, —just on the threshold of life." He went about his business of being a spiritual philosopher with a directness and sincerity that won respect. Thoreau found his attitude "one of greater faith and expectation than that of any man I know." Alcott was the first resident of Concord to be put in jail for conscientious refusal to pay a tax in support of a government he considered unjust; and Sam Staples, the local constable, who was later to lock up Thoreau on a similar charge, declared, "I vum, I believe it was nothing but principle, for I never heerd a man talk honester." Where principle was concerned Alcott demonstrated on several occasions that he did not know the name of fear. Nor was he afraid to earn his living on occasion by menial labor. Thoreau found his ideas indefinite and undisciplined, yet was unwilling to cavil at his impracticality. "The feelers of his thought diverge,—such is the breadth of their grasp,—not converge; and in his society almost alone I can express at my leisure, with more or less success, my vaguest but most cherished fancy or thought. There are never any obstacles in the way of our meeting. He has no creed. He is not pledged to any institution. The sanest man I ever knew; the fewest crotchets, after all, has he." At the end of the chapter on "Winter Visitors" in *Walden* may be found Thoreau's considered tribute to the least worldly of philosophers.

Alcott's crotchets did not escape the amused notice of his irreverent friend, who found it incongruous that the genealogy of the Alcock family should absorb so much of the sage's interest,—"he whom only the genealogy of humanity, the descent of man from God should concern!" The rustic summerhouse that Alcott constructed in Emerson's garden also awakened Thoreau's mind to derision. But the two men shared too many loyalties to have any serious falling out.

Alcott on his part early acknowledged the spiritual kinship of the younger man, but in terms that derogated nothing from his independence. "Emerson, Miss Fuller, Thoreau, and myself," he wrote in 1846," are the only persons who treat things in the new spirit, each working distinct veins in the same mine of Being." He perceived at once the poetic quality of Thoreau's mind, but considered his a "walking" (he did not say pedestrian) Muse. "But this fits him all the better for his special task of delineating these yet unspoiled American things, and of inspiring us with a sense of their homelier beauties—opening to us the riches of a nation scarcely yet discovered by her own population." Admiring and perceptive comments on Thoreau's writing and conversation are thickly scattered through the pages of Alcott's journal. Perhaps the most condensed appraisal is this, written in 1859:

"He is less thinker than observer; a naturalist in tendency but of a mystic habit, and a genius for detecting the essence in the form and giving forth the soul of things seen. He knows more of Nature's secrets than any man I have known, and of Man as related to Nature. He thinks and sees for himself in ways eminently original, and is formidably individual and persistent."

Alcott was often accused of having his head in the clouds, but he saw things on earth with extremely clear vision. Practically all the things that are important to say about Thoreau are contained in his journal.

With other Concord writers Thoreau was acquainted, though his shyness kept him from reaching anything like intimacy, except with one or two. He and Margaret Fuller learned much from each other. Hawthorne, who bought Thoreau's boat and rechristened it the "Pond-Lily," was a more distant friend, accustomed to move in a different social sphere. The man who came nearest to becoming a companion of Thoreau's later years was the poet William Ellery Channing, the namesake of the well-known Unitarian clergyman and the husband of Margaret Fuller's sister. But Channing, though an admirable partner on what he called their *riparial* excursions along the river, was intellectually of flimsy stuff. He never managed to make even one passably good poem, though he could sometimes produce an arresting phrase. Thoreau called his way of writing the "sublimo-slipshod style," and thought it would be good discipline for him to write in Latin, "for then he would be compelled to say something always, and frequently have recourse to his grammar and dictionary." Edgar Allan Poe mercilessly dissected his failings in a review full of animus against the New England "school" of writers.

Other men, too, many of them younger, came to know

Thoreau through his books and articles and to occupy a station between that of friends and disciples. Among them were Harrison Blake and Theodore Brown of Worcester, Daniel Ricketson of New Bedford, Edward Hoar of Concord, Thomas Cholmondeley the English visitor, and Horace Mann, Jr., who accompanied Thoreau on his last long journey to Minnesota. There were many who delighted to share his walks on occasion and to join him in serious reflection, for though Thoreau has written vehemently of the joys of solitude and self-sufficiency he was not indifferent to the pleasures of companionship with his peers. But let the companions come one at a time, so that there might be a true exchange of thoughts, not a mere bandying of compliments.

Alcott, who so often spoke the definitive word about Thoreau, may appropriately offer a final definition of the kind of response he aroused in those who best knew him: "I should say he inspired love, if indeed the sentiment he awakens did not seem to partake of something yet purer, if that were possible, and as yet nameless from its rarity and excellency."

7

Life in the Village

Airplane pilots have commonly remarked that merely by flying high among the clouds they acquire an extraordinary detachment from the concerns of men on the ground. They have an intoxicating feeling of superabundant power, of room to expand in all directions. They are released from the pressure of the crowd, and forthwith they are no longer afflicted by the worries and apprehensions of life at the customary level.

Thoreau attained somewhat the same detached point of view in regard to human affairs, not by soaring above the earth, but by identifying himself with the earth and its various natural phenomena more closely than the average man is likely to do. The earth was his airplane swung in space. The planets were his neighbors. His mind was so occupied with moon and stars, clouds and winds, swamps and woods and their inhabitants that he had little time to bother about what his human neighbors were doing. Toward them and their affairs in fact he adopted a slightly quizzical attitude which can hardly have increased his popularity with the majority of Concord citizens. His opinion of their importance was obviously low, and he had an irritating forthrightness in saying so. They seemed to him to swarm like ants by his woodpile or tadpoles at the pond's edge. As he put it in *Walden*: "In one direction from my house there was a colony of muskrats in the river meadows; under the grove of elms and buttonwoods in the other horizon was a village of busy men, as curious to me as if they had been prairie-dogs, each sitting at the mouth of its burrow, or running over to a neighbor's to gossip. I went there frequently to observe their habits."

The relations between Thoreau and the villagers were

often little better than an armed truce. His way of life was a criticism of theirs. His negations challenged their scheme of values. Emerson summed it up in a striking if slightly exaggerated sentence: "He was bred to no profession; he never married; he lived alone; he never went to church; he never voted; he refusd to pay a tax to the State; he ate no flesh, he drank no wine, he never knew the use of tobacco; and, though a naturalist, he used neither trap nor gun." Considering what human sensibilities are, it speaks well for Concord that Thoreau was even tolerated. Many resented and ridiculed him, many regarded his supposed shiftlessness as a scandal. When on one occasion a campfire got away from him and burned over a tract of woodland, it was only the lucky circumstance that the son of Judge Hoar was with him and equally guilty that saved Thoreau from vigorous reprisals. For years afterward he was not allowed to forget that he was the man who set the woods afire.

Yet once Thoreau's wide divergence from conventional attitudes of mind is realized, it is necessary to add immediately that he expressed his radicalism far more in words than in action. It is only in comparison with Emerson that he seems a doer rather than a thinker. He was not anti-social, though he favored a stringent revision of social values. And above all, his opinions were not those of a misfit or a failure. When he chose to do so he could adapt himself to ordinary standards. It was several times within his power to be what his neighbors would have considered successful. His early venture at keeping a private school was prospering until his brother's failing health put an end to it. The pencils that the family manufactured were of superior quality, and the plumbago, ground by a secret float-process invented by Thoreau and his father, was the finest that lithographers could obtain. If he had cared to devote his time and energy to the pencil business, he could almost certainly have developed a thriving trade. He was also a competent surveyor, and found as much to do in that way as he wished to undertake. And finally in the unremunerative profession of authorship, where few Americans of his generation were able to make a living without resorting to other callings, Thoreau worked out as successful a *modus vivendi* as anyone and before he died in middle age had published a book that was distinctly a success by commercial standards. It is impossible, therefore, to dismiss Thoreau as an embittered failure.

In *Walden,* when he announces that he is addressing primarily those of his countrymen who are dissatisfied with their lot and don't know what to do about it, Thoreau is careful to dissociate himself from the discontented and to reckon himself among "those who find their encouragement and inspiration in precisely the present condition of things, and cherish it with the fondness and enthusiasm of lovers"— at least this is where he thinks he belongs "to some extent." It would not be easy to cast doubt on Thoreau's sincere attachment to the place of his birth. In spite of the faults he saw in Concord, he was willing to present himself with the freedom of the village.

Nevertheless this indigenous New Englander was a persistent critic of what the universal Yankee nation most prided itself upon and worshipped, its increasing material prosperity and its progress in mechanical invention. By 1845 the industrial revolution was in full swing in the northeastern section of the United States. Steamboats were running, railroads were being built, textile mills were in full operation, the electric telegraph was being extended, and the successful laying of a cable between France and England forecast the Atlantic cable to come a decade later. Except for the regression caused by the financial panic of 1837, wealth was increasing and the standard of living was steadily advancing. Who could look upon these multiplied wonders as anything but unalloyed benefits? Only a few perfectionists and cranks such as Emerson, who declared that

> "Things are in the saddle
> And ride mankind,"

and, of course, Thoreau, who persisted in describing all modern inventions as improved means to unimproved ends.

Thoreau's transcendental economics was not concerned with wealth as understood on the stock exchange. As he figured it, the fundamental questions were: What kind of life is a man enabled to lead? How much of his time is consumed by distasteful drudgery incident to earning a living merely? What margin has he left for doing the things that he really wants to do? Thoreau did not feel (and here many plain people who enjoy the occupations whereby they earn their livings may disagree with him) that time spent in providing the necessaries of life could possibly be as well invested as free time. Consequently, if all his waking hours were to be used up in earning his living, he would consider his life a blank. His problem was to secure as large a portion of time as possible for voluntary occupations. The richest man by his scheme of values would be the one who could devote the greatest amount of time to his own affairs. Thoreau is assuming, of course, that his economic man is high-minded and will not choose to waste his spangle of existence in riot and indulgence.

The test of value that he applied to any item that might be included in the apparatus of living was, therefore, determined by the question: How much life is required to be exchanged for it, either immediately or in the long run? In Thoreau's opinion the comforts, conveniences, and luxuries of civilized living had so multiplied that many men virtually made slaves of themselves in the effort to secure them, or to keep up the properties that they supposedly owned, but which in reality possessed them. His first suggestion to those who were discouraged in the struggle was to simplify their lives by seeing how much they could manage to do without.

This was a solution that he found eminently satisfactory in his own practice, and in *Walden* he describes with an elaborate parody of economic statistics his not too serious demonstration that the problem of earning a living need occupy only a small fraction of the time, if a man is young, unburdened with a family, in good health, and not eager to encumber himself with many possessions. This "experiment" in the art of simple living is partly a burlesque, put forward with tongue in cheek. Thoreau did not even adopt it for himself as a permanent way of living. But the advice to center one's aims in something other than material possessions is earnestly meant.

Thoreau perceived at once that an economic system based on sheer acquisitiveness could not lead to the beneficent effects that current theory claimed would flow from it. The inhuman conditions that workers had to face in British mines and mills before working conditions became subject to government regulation were notorious in the United States, and it was hoped that such brutality might be avoided here. The managers of the textile mills at Lowell, for example, took pains to provide proper housing for the girls they employed and to see that the operatives were not driven to the limit of their endurance, even though they spent a twelve-and-a-half-hour day at the looms. They encouraged the formation of "improvement circles," and were proud of the literary magazine called the *Lowell Offering* which the young women conducted without outside assistance. To Whittier, who wrote a series of journalistic articles collected in 1845 as *The Stranger in Lowell,* it seemed that the American industrial experiment was avoiding the worst mistakes of the British and was a marvel of efficient economic organization.

In Thoreau's opinion, however, production for profit was vitiated at the start by the low motives that inspired it. "I cannot believe," he wrote, "that our factory system is the best mode by which men may get clothing. The condition of the operatives is becoming every day more like that of the English; and it cannot be wondered at, since, as far as I have heard or observed, the principal object is, not that mankind may be well and honestly clad, but, unquestionably, that the corporations may be enriched. In the long run men hit only what they aim at. Therefore, though they should fail immediately, they had better aim at something high."

For similar reasons Thoreau looked upon railroads with suspicion, and amused himself by making somewhat specious calculations to show that a man who traveled afoot could cover as much ground as one who must first earn his carfare by working as a common laborer at a dollar a day. It was not so much that he resented the intrusion of the locomotive into his solitude at Walden Pond; that he found companionable. But he distrusted mechanical improvements as irrelevant to the main issue, which was the improvement of the quality of human living. He could not overlook the exploitation of the miserable Irish immigrants by whose toil the railroad was built. And to what end was all this toiling and wretchedness? Few readers of *Walden* will fail to recall Thoreau's gibe at the project of "tunneling under the Atlantic" in order that America may know instantly that the Princess Adelaide has the whooping-cough. There was nothing in Thoreau's disposition to match that elation which Whitman so clearly felt in contemplating the triumphs of mechanical ingenuity:

"The seas inlaid with eloquent gentle wires!"

Whitman was the more modern in accepting uncritically such watchwords of the nineteenth century as science and progress. Thoreau insisted with old-fashioned caution on examining at once their bearing on man's welfare.

To him the problem of improving society was a matter of self-improvement many times multiplied. Let every man live up to his highest possibilities and there would be no need to worry about the state of the nation. Anything other than

ution in himself—a more than '76—having got
igning to the doing it out fully." Ideally Thoreau
d to go beyond the saying that that government
n governs least and to state flatly that that government
est which governs not at all. But if man's present
tions demanded some form of regulation, con-
ld extend only to the establishment of a kind of
l service.

s called "Civil Disobedience" and "Life without
n which Thoreau's views are asserted without
, are landmarks of an unfashionable and perhaps
adicalism. They are not reconcilable with Social-
nism, or any modern program for the conversion
o a classless basis through the domination of a
do not contemplate the fusion of individuals into
the hammering of masses into pressure-groups
Nevertheless they have not been without effect,
vorld which seems to be discarding as rapidly as
oreau's basic philosophy. "Civil Disobedience,"
ble political agitator among the Hindoo workers
frica, bore strange fruit in Gandhi's powerful
passive resistance. The chapter called "Economy"
became a minor gospel of the British Labor Party
its uncompromising emphasis, not on reform, but
ng at once to realize the ultimate values of life
ng only for them. "I came into this world, not
ake this a good place to live in, but to live in it,
r bad," wrote Thoreau. He belived in having his
mortality now. One man thoroughly imbued with
tions is a force to be reckoned with. Several such
constitute a silent revolution.

ceivable that a resurgence of religious conviction
e men's wills in a passionate determination to make
ail in human affairs. The enormous force of in
d fanatical resolution which is now commonl

individual improvement was beside the point. Hence Thoreau's sturdy independence was revolted by humanitarian projects for doing good to one's fellow-men, and to the subject of philanthropy he devoted some of his most astringent comments. He understood completely the degradation of being pawed over by a would-be benefactor. Let the charitable keep their hands off. The best service that he could render to mankind lay, he thought, in developing his specific talents to the height of his capacity. Even in preaching and practicing simplicity he did not aim at starting a movement. "To what end do I lead a simple life at all, pray? That I may teach others to simplify their lives?—and so all our lives be *simplified* merely, like an algebraic formula? Or not, rather, that I may make use of the ground I have cleared, to live more worthily and profitably?"

From what has been said it can easily be seen that Thoreau's ideas of how social conditions might be ameliorated were directly opposite to the techniques of social service as practiced at the present time. The basis of his thinking was religious, rooted in the Puritan conception of man's responsibility to God for the disposal of his talents. Man became his brother's keeper most effectually when by means of his own self-fulfillment he set a high standard for others to live up to. What we should labor to do unto others is to impart the courage of our example. The essence of Thoreau's social philosophy may be summed up in the following two quotations from his personal letters:

"Happy the man who observes the heavenly and the terrestrial law in just proportion; whose every faculty, from the soles of his feet to the crown of his head, obeys the law of its level; who neither stoops nor goes on tiptoe, but lives a balanced life, acceptable to nature and to God."

"Do not be too moral. You may cheat yourself out of much life so. Aim above morality. Be not simply good; be good for something."

manipulated for the gaining of political or economic advantage might thus be turned to helpful social uses. If this should happen, Thoreau would at once be recognized as a prophet who prepared the way. The final defeat of demogogue and dictator occurs when no one can be found to think them important.

The creaky operation of government and politics in Massachusetts seemed to Thoreau less worthy of interest than the perfect functioning of muskrat society on the Concord meadows and the timeless mysteries of the seasons. But if the administration of human affairs interfered with the cosmic duties of citizens, or if the degradation of the state humiliated them by outraging their sense of justice, then the state had to be attended to. Otherwise it did not deserve to occupy a man's thought.

The issue of negro slavery was a case in point. Thoreau did not wish to have any truck with the foul institution, but it would not leave him alone. He was forced to consider it, and having considered it to condemn it, and having condemned it to take action. The Thoreau house was a well-recognized station on the underground railroad, and on at least one occasion Henry himself convoyed a fugitive slave on his way to Canada.

Emerson, it will be recalled, was unwilling to enlist as an anti-slavery agitator, partly because he had to guard his none too robust health, but partly also because he regarded slavery as only one monstrous symptom of the corruption at the heart of society which he was trying to combat by intellectual and spiritual means. Yet when the Fugitive Slave Law was passed, early in 1850, Emerson's reserve was broken and he entered in his journal a white-hot resolve, the most furious words that ever came from his pen: "This filthy enactment was made in the nineteenth century, by people who could read and write. I will not obey it, by God."

Thoreau, like Alcott, had reached a similar stage of intransigence at a considerably earlier date, and his response to an offense against his sense of right and wrong was uncompromising. He had discovered the pattern of dissent that he was to follow later, when in 1838 he "signed off" from the village church and refused to pay his tax for the support of the minister. There remained still a long list of institutions from which he would prefer to sign off. The war with Mexico, even if it were not inspired as most northern idealists believed it was by a desire to extend slave territory, was in his eyes an unrighteous war. "When . . . a whole country is unjustly overrun and conquered by a foreign army, and subjected to military law, I think that it is not too soon for honest men to rebel and revolutionize," he wrote, and added by way of pay-off: "What makes this duty the more urgent is the fact that the country so overrun is not our own, but ours is the invading army." His method of rebelling was more drastic than the making of any number of pacifist speeches would have been. Thoreau as a sovereign political entity seceded from the state of Massachusetts by ostentatiously neglecting to pay his poll-tax. As a consequence, he spent one night in jail. A friend intervened by paying the tax, and in the morning he was released.

The famous story that Emerson accompanied the jailer to the door of the cell and that gazing reprovingly on the delinquent he remarked, "Henry, why are you here?" only to have Thoreau reply with blazing indignation, "Waldo, why are you *not* here?" is probably apocryphal. It seems to be true, however, that Emerson at first deplored Thoreau's action as "in bad taste," but before the month was out he was comparing Webster's truckling to the politicians with Thoreau's uncompromising firmness. "My friend Mr. Thoreau has gone to jail rather than pay his tax. On him they could not calculate."

It was characteristic of the two men that, if we may judge by what they confided to their journals, Emerson was more disturbed by the passage of the Fugitive Slave Law and Thoreau by the concrete application of it in the forcible return to slavery of certain colored residents of Boston, notably by the seizure of Anthony Burns. Thoreau could not say enough to express his contempt for the compliant officials of the State who permitted an injustice to be enacted under the sanction of a national statute. "Every man in New England," he wrote, "capable of the sentiment of patriotism must have lived the last three weeks with the sense of having suffered a vast, indefinite loss . . . I feel that, to some extent, the State has fatally interfered with my just and proper business. It has not merely interrupted me in my passage through Court Street on errands of trade, but it has, to some extent, interrupted me and every man on his onward and upward path, on which he had trusted soon to leave Court Street far behind." And his counsel was again that of a confirmed comeouter: "My advice to the State is simply this: to dissolve her union with the slaveholder instantly. She can find no respectable law or precedent which sanctions its continuance. And to each inhabitant of Massachusetts, to dissolve his union with the State, as long as she hesitates to do her duty."

All that Thoreau had ever said in contempt of a government that paltered with moral issues pales before the words that he uttered when the one man who dared to assault the very stronghold of a great wrong lay wounded and awaiting death on the gallows. Old John Brown of Kansas had visited Concord in March, 1857, and had taken meals at Thoreau's house. His homely rustic manners and simple directness had strongly appealed to Thoreau, who could recognize a man when he saw one. Early in October, 1859, Brown was again in Concord to secure funds that his supporters had been collecting for him. From there he proceeded directly to conduct his raid on Harper's Ferry. The news of his immortal failure shocked the nation, and the first response even of northern abolitionists was to disown Brown's act. He was attacked in the press and from the pulpit as a misguided and insane fanatic, who had succeeded only in making mischief.

Less than two weeks after the raid, and while the country was still seething with indignation, Thoreau announced to his neighbors that he intended to speak in behalf of John Brown the next Sunday evening in the Town Hall of Concord. To some who sought to dissaude him he replied sharply that he had not asked for their advice but for their presence to hear what he had to say. Before a large audience he delivered his "Plea for Captain John Brown," the most forthright of his utterances. It was not, as its title might suggest, an appeal for clemency for the old fighter. It was the vindication of the character of a hero by a man who shared the same qualities of straightforwardness and independence. Two days later Thoreau read the same speech in Boston, and the day following in Worcester.

Seldom has a magnanimous deed been more nobly interpreted. Thoreau perceived at once the moral force of Brown's example. Here was the antidote to the long course of shuffling evasion that politicians had been pursuing. "For once we are lifted out of the trivialness and dust of politics into the region of truth and manhood." He reviewed Brown's character and personal history, contrasting his courage and the generosity of his aims with the apathy and caution that editors, clergy, and other public men had everywhere exhibited. The Day of Judgment for Massachusetts was at hand. "No man in America has ever stood up so persistently and effectively for the dignity of human nature, knowing himself for a man, and the equal of any and all governments."

Thoreau took part, with Emerson, Alcott, and others, in the services held at Concord on December 2, the day of John Brown's execution, and a little later he recorded in his journal a passage which contains the gist of his final tribute to the completest man he had ever known, a warrior-saint whose heroic stature matched Cromwell's in his imagination: "On the day of his translation, I heard, to be sure, that he was hung, but I did not know what that meant,—and I felt no sorrow on his account; but not for a day or two did I even *hear* that he was dead, and not after any number of days shall I believe it. Of all the men who are said to be my contemporaries, it seems to me that John Brown is the only one who *has not* died. I meet him at every turn. He is more alive than ever he was. He is not confined to North Elba [where he was buried] nor to Kansas. He is no longer working in secret only. John Brown has earned immortality."

The American tradition is rich in the memorable sayings of our statesmen which have lived in popular esteem long after the occasions that gave rise to them. "Give me liberty or give me death!" . . . "All men are created free and equal" . . . "government of the people, by the people, for the people." But nothing Jefferson or Lincoln ever said is more inherently American or deserves to be more deeply engraved on the minds of a free people than a sentence wrung from Thoreau in the agony of his sympathetic comprehension of what John Brown had died for:

"The only government that I recognize—and it matters not how few are at the head of it, or how small its army—is that power that establishes justice in the land, never that which establishes injustice."

9

Understanding Nature

Defiance of American orthodoxy and respectability was endemic among finer spirits of the nineteenth century, particularly among men of letters. Emerson, Poe, Hawthorne, Melville, and Whitman were all at odds with the world as they found it. Emerson in early resigning from his pulpit, Hawthorne in joining the social reformers at Brook Farm, Melville in shipping on a whaler, each in his separate way was testifying to a sense of alienation from a society more and more standardized and dominated by material concerns.

No protest was more dramatic than Thoreau's. In the opinion of a recent student of Melville, the late William Ellery Sedgwick: "It is as if the long process of revolt which originated in England in the seventeenth century and was carried forward by successive generations of Puritans and pioneers, which dissented from the Church of England and broke away from the British government, came to a climax when Thoreau turned his back on civilization and went to live alone at Walden Pond." If it seems fantastic to suppose that a process of such proportions should culminate in an event of such small consequence, we may recall, following the way of analogy dear to the transcendentalists, that the significance of a mountain's peak is not due to its area as compared with the size of its base. The logic of Calvinism and Democracy alike pointed to the symbolic figure of a plain man with his feet on earth and his head among the stars.

In setting up a communion of saints in the American wilderness the Puritan founders of New England accepted an ideal very different from that involved in establishing a government for all sorts and conditions of men. A government theoretically intended to include everybody must be adjusted to a catholic conception of human nature, while a communion of saints implies drastic exclusions. Though Puritan clergy and magistrates liked to argue that they had not left the Church of England but had only separated themselves from its errors, the distinction seemed immaterial to Anglicans who found themselves banished from Massachusetts Bay. Somehow a line had been drawn and men were required to toe the mark. In spite of occasional politic relentings such as the adoption of the "half-way covenant" to permit unconverted but substantial Christians to become members of the Puritan church, the policy of Calvinism was inherently exclusive. It magnified the small group of the elect, the Gideon's band who could show evidence that they were indeed chosen of God.

Democracy likewise, and paradoxically enough, was not available for all men. Born of the Protestant revolt against the traditional order, it commended itself to vigorous radicals as a method of discarding institutions which had become encumbrances. Democracy was justified in view of the dilapidations committed in its name. In one of his most cryptic sentences Melville remarked that, "Democracy lops, lops." The process of stripping government of its outworn trappings, however, could be carried out only as long as the citizenry remained alert and militant. Only the strenuous could keep Democracy from degeneration.

The winnowing implied in both Calvinism and Democracy might lead ultimately to profound spiritual isolation. The communion of saints, refined by successive purges, could in the end resolve itself into a community of one. Or in the political sphere the standard of fitness in the body politic might be raised until the majority of those fit to rule consisted of no more than Luther's "one with God." Sensitive men in nineteenth century America were becoming increasingly aware of the tendencies making for individual isolation. The thought of aloofness was dreadful to Hawthorne and he constantly recurred to it in his stories. Both Melville and

Thoreau were obliged to cope with the same specter. Captain Ahab in *Moby Dick,* like the Puritan spirit constantly discarding appliances and rejecting human sympathies in his fanatical desire to pursue and grapple with the white whale of universal mystery, is an incarnation of loneliness. Melville, however, after following his thought to a dead end of disillusionment, recoiled and gradually recovered. Thoreau, who experienced no powerful revulsion of feeling, dallied with solitude until his death.

Two quotations from the journal for the summer of 1852 show that Thoreau was beginning to feel that his closeness to nature was cutting him off from human associations. The first entry is admonitory: "Nature must be viewed humanly to be viewed at all; that is, her scenes must be associated with humane affections, such as are associated with one's native place, for instance. She is most significant to a lover. A lover of Nature is preeminently a lover of man. If I have no friend, what is Nature to me? She ceases to be morally significant." Only a month or two later seclusion is announced as an accepted fact. "By my intimacy with nature I find myself withdrawn from man. My interest in the sun and the moon, in the morning and the evening, compels me to solitude." Thoreau's resignation to loneliness might be called stoical if he had not been so vocal about it.

His chapter on "Solitude" in *Walden* is a masterpiece of extravagance compounded of paradox and romantic fallacies. "Why should I feel lonely? is not our planet in the Milky Way?" "I find it wholesome to be alone the greater part of the time . . . I never found the companion that was so companionable as solitude. We are for the most part more lonely when we go among men than when we stay in our chambers." "Society is commonly too cheap . . . We meet at meals three times a day, and give each other a new taste of that old musty cheese that we are." "I am no more lonely than the loon on the pond that laughs so loud, or than Walden Pond itself . . . I am no more lonely than a single mullein or dandelion in a pasture, or a bean leaf, or sorrel, or a horse-fly, or a humblebee. I am no more lonely than the Mill Brook, or a weathercock, or the north star, or the south wind, or an April shower, or a January thaw, or the first spider in a new house." A truce to similitudes! Is this the Thoreau who as a young man burst into tears at the mere thought of leaving his home and family?

A note of false sentimentality very infrequent in Thoreau's writing occurs at the end of this same chapter where he personifies external nature as "an elderly dame . . . invisible to most persons, in whose odorous herb garden I love to stroll sometimes, gathering simples and listening to her fables." The enjoyment of solitude depended in a measure on the fancied sympathy of the out-of-door world. For a time the companionship of nature seemed a happy substitute for the more exacting association with men and women, and so Thoreau's isolation was at once deepened and made to seem tolerable. If we may trust certain entries in his journal that become more numerous toward the end, Thoreau was increasingly aware of a growing impoverishment and emptiness in his life. It is doubtful if he ever realized explicitly that worship of nature is only a thinly disguised form of self-worship, leading to sterility. Walking and boating trips had always been a part of his life before he exalted them into a chief concern. By the time he perceived that the path he was following did not lead where he wanted to go, it was too late to change. His quest for a free, abundant life ended in his being committed to comradeship with rocks and stones and trees. There is a trace of defiance in his later comments on his situation, as for example the following: "My work is writing, and I do not hesitate, though I know that no subject is too trivial for me, tried by ordinary standards; for, ye fools, the theme is nothing, the life is everything. All that interests the reader is the depth and intensity of the life excited . . .

That is, man is all in all, Nature nothing, but as she draws him out and reflects him."

There were two levels in Thoreau's attitude toward nature, and his shifting from one to the other leads to frequent inconsistencies. As a country-bred boy he had ranged the woods with his brother, deeply absorbing the healthy animal joys of fishing and hunting and camping out. Later in life memories of these rambles were associated with the closest human intimacy that he had ever known. His excursions also supplied him with the raw material for the making of essays, and after all he was primarily a writer. Hence Thoreau insisted on saving a generous portion of every day for trips afield. His delight in these jaunts was exquisite and wholesome, if still somewhat boyish.

But his preference for nature also rested on transcendental theorizing. His intense enjoyment of outdoor life led him to accept without hesitation the rhapsodic and reckless glorification of nature and of nature's beneficent influence on man, of which Emerson, outdoing Wordsworth, had made himself a major prophet. Emerson had missed the *caveat* which Coleridge, disillusioned after his early raptures, addressed to his brother poet:

> "O William! We receive but what we give,
> And in our life alone does Nature live."

Possessed by his mystical confidence in the immanence of the universal spirit in nature as well as in man, Emerson could see God in the meanest of inanimate objects. "What is there of the divine in a load of bricks? What is there of the divine in a barber's shop? . . . Much. All." The enthusiast found no difficulty in perceiving in the pleasanter aspects of nature a power to confirm the soul's health and to discipline the moral sense. The laws of spirit seemed to merge into one system with the laws of matter, and the ancient precept, Know Thyself, became identical with the modern slogan, Study nature.

76

As a poet Emerson, like Wordsworth, was capable of imposing serenely ethical interpretations on natural phenomena, sometimes with tonic effect, but as a thinker he was essentially uncritical of ideas that commended themselves to his blandly optimistic temper. Speaking of Emerson's philosophy of nature Professor Joseph Warren Beach observes: "Must we not admit that it is, for the most part, a loose and popular rendering of Coleridge, who gives a loose and popular rendering of (mainly) Schelling, who—for all his magnificent show of dialectic—is no better than a Kant run wild."

Thoreau, whose element was excess, carried the transcendental personalizing of nature even further than Emerson. What the Puritans had regarded as the garment darkly veiling God's majesty, and what Emerson had celebrated as a flowing revelation of the Over-Soul, he wholeheartedly took to his bosom as "friend" and "bride." Nature could give him the perfect response, the complete toleration that he could not expect from men and women. Nature demanded nothing in return. "If I am too cold for human friendship," he wrote in 1852, "I trust I shall not soon be too cold for natural influences. It appears to be a law that you cannot have a deep sympathy with both man and nature. Those qualities which bring you near to the one estrange you from the other." Association with human beings, in other words, checks a tendency to unimpeded expansion of the ego, but nature leaves one gloriously free: free but unchallenged, unprovoked to supreme effort, not subject to criticism.

Thoreau, even while passionately identifying himself with nature, seems to have felt that something was amiss: I seem to be more constantly merged in nature; my intellectual life is more obedient to nature than formerly, but perchance less obedient to spirit. I have less memorable seasons. I exact less of myself." But he did not stay to analyze his difficulties. "The meaning of Nature," as Emerson noted, "was never attempted to be defined by him." A greater assimilation either of Christian doctrine or of the spirit of the Greek and Roman classics might have preserved him from the bacchic excesses of transcendentalism; but Christianity was obscured for him by his dislike for its institutions and the ineptitude of its ministers, and with the passing years his reading of the classics grew less frequent. Though he cherished independence of mind, he was not independent enough to scrutinize with appropriate skepticism the romantic doctrines of the benefits of solitude and the kindliness of nature.

It is significant, pathetically so, that Thoreau made much of a remarkable echo that he encountered while surveying the Hunt farm. After days of unimportant drudgery with stupid companions, he says, here was "somebody I could talk with." When it is said that in devoting himself to nature Thoreau was "pursuing perfection in a vacuum," it should be added that the vacuum was not altogether of his own making.

There was one important difference between Emerson's attitude toward nature and Thoreau's, a difference that suggests one of the channels by which the too placid accumulations of transcendental speculation might ultimately be drained off. Emerson, who went to nature chiefly for mental refreshment, held the world of woods and streams generally at arm's length. He was satisfied to theorize about nature in general terms. Thoreau, on the other hand, could never saturate his senses enough with the concrete and specific items from nature's store. His journal for the last ten years of his life reads like a vast inventory, often tediously detailed, often repetitious. But there is this to say for it, that it points away from the conception of nature as a projection of universal mind in matter. It testifies to an implicit conviction of the separateness of the inner and outer worlds, to a respect for the unspoiled integrity of the latter, to a suspicion that even the transcendental temperament might profit by "the discipline of looking always at what is to be seen."

Thoreau was not a scientist, and his persistent measuring of the girth of trees, the height of floods, the thickness of ice, and so on would be dismaying in their clumsiness if regarded as attempts to collect scientific data. But probably they were not that. They were the awkward caresses that Thoreau lavished on the one consuming love of his life. He simply could not know enough of the world around him. If he was at rare intervals a visionary, he lived most commonly in the almost savage delicacy of his senses. He guarded them carefully from blunting by overstimulation. Fair Nature, which demanded no hard service, smiled upon him and he responded by recording in innumerable pages every least shade of expression on her countenance. He found his true vocation in being the enamored prose-poet of the countryside.

10

Literary Artistry

Thoreau was inclined to simplify the business of writing as well as the business of living. Toward the close of the year 1841, when he was still thinking of himself as a poet rather than a prose writer, he adopted in extreme form the idea of the poet's community with other men. "Good poetry," he declared, "seems so simple and natural a thing that when we meet it we wonder that all men are not always poets. Poetry is nothing but healthy speech." Prose, he was later to discover, was also nothing but healthy speech with the weight of a man's full conviction behind it. In 1859, when he was deeply stirred by the John Brown affair, he reasserted a conception essentially Miltonic that good writing "demands earnestness and manhood chiefly" and is a matter of plain integrity. All else is mere flummery. "Literary gentlemen, editors, and critics think that they know how to write because they have studied grammar and rhetoric; but they are egregiously mistaken. The *art* of composition is as simple as the discharge of a bullet from a rifle, and its masterpieces imply an infinitely greater force behind them . . . It suggests that the one great rule of composition—and if I were a professor of rhetoric I should insist on this—is to *speak the truth*. This first, this second, this third; pebbles in your mouth or not."

The tone of depreciation that he employed in speaking of mere literary craftsmanship is occasionally repeated. When Thoreau noticed in turning over the biographical sketches in *Homes of American Authors* that many of the New England group had at one time or another contributed to the *North American Review*, he asserted at once, "It is one of my qualifications that I have not written an article for the *North American Review*." As Emerson explained when he first mentioned Thoreau to Carlyle: "There is a universal timidity, conformity, and rage; and on the other hand the most resolute realism in the young." Thoreau typified youth in revolt. Like Emily Dickinson he found it impossible to speak the truth within the decorous literary conventions of late romanticism and the genteel tradition. He was groping his way toward a technique of sincerity beyond anything that his literary contemporaries had yet grasped.

As an experimental poet he met a defeat attributable to two causes. The first was his own uncertainty, not of aims, but of means; the second was the failure of even the most friendly readers to perceive the basis on which he was working. Even Emerson, who shared in theory many of Thoreau's principles, did not see how close the young poet was coming to realizing them in practice. People were obsessed by literary tradition. Ultimately it took the robust self-confidence of a Walt Whitman to burst through the net of convention. Thoreau's confidence wavered. His poems, when some specimens were published in the *Dial,* were too radical for the public taste and were ridiculed by the uncomprehending for their "ragged and halting lines." Later he gave a number of his pieces, or fragments chipped from them, a setting in the pages of the *Week,* but there too they remained unappreciated. On the advice of Emerson he burned the bulk of his early poems. At the end of his life he looked back on this action with regret. Perhaps, he surmised, the poems were not as bad as they had thought them twenty years before.

His final opinion was indeed prescient. Though his contemporaries considered that his poems "lacked lyrical fire and melodious utterance," it has at long last been perceived that they possess other and more interesting qualities. After noting that Thoreau's search for a satisfactory poetic style led him to range over an unusual variety of models—the Greek anthology, Horace, the medieval mystery plays, Skelton, Ben Jonson, Herbert, Thomson and Cowper, Blake and Wordsworth—Professor Henry W. Wells, who has made the only competent critical study of the complete poems, comes to the conclusion that the largest number of his most memorable pieces have no specific connection with the past but in a remarkable way anticipate the poetry of the present moment. "Thoreau, like Emily Dickinson or Baudelaire, anticipates the bold symbolism, airy impressionism, stringent realism, and restless inconsistencies of twentieth-century poetry." And again: "Thoreau's breadth of vision is precisely what our own age, tragically seeking a new consolidation of mankind, most of all requires." The one thing his poetry seldom does is to lapse into the facile sentimentalism and smooth nullity characteristic of the nineteenth-century imitators of such fashionable models as Byron and Tennyson.

It is possible to regret the loss of Thoreau's youthful poems without deploring his early change to prose writing. He did not feel with Matthew Arnold that any lowering of intention was involved. "Great prose of equal elevation," he thought, "commands our respect more than great verse, since it implies a more permanent and level height, a life more pervaded with the grandeur of thought. The poet only makes an irruption, like a Parthian, and is off again, shooting while he retreats; but the prose writer has conquered, like a Roman, and settled colonies." The instrument of prose was well suited to his genius, and within its broader scope he could employ the powerful concision and quick responsiveness that distinguished his poetry.

What Thoreau aimed at from first to last in all his writing was the expression of ultimate truth or reality. "You may rely on it that you have the best of me in my books," he wrote to a young inquirer during his last illness, "and that I am not worth seeing personally . . . what am I to the truth I feebly utter?" One of the most vigorous passages in *Walden* states his determination to penetrate through all shams and illusions to the very heart of actuality. "Let us settle ourselves, and work and wedge our feet downward through the mud and slush of opinion, and prejudice, and tradition, and delusion and appearance, that alluvion which covers the globe, . . . through church and state, through poetry and philosophy and religion, till we come to a hard bottom and rocks in place, which we can call *reality,* and say, This is, and no mistake; and then begin, having a *point d'appui,* below freshet and frost and fire . . . Be it life or death, we crave only reality." Eloquent as these words are, they do not tell us how and by what tests Thoreau proposed to distinguish what was real from what was appearance or delusion. Perhaps like jesting Pilate on a famous occasion he was more interested in asking, What is truth? than in staying for an answer.

He seems to have recognized in practice, however, two sorts of reality, one of which he called "poetry" and the other "fact." The first consisted of an inward and overwhelming vitality of conviction, the second of a minute faithfulness to the external world. Theoretically the two seemed entirely distinct, yet he found that they tended to overlap. "I have a commonplace-book for facts and another for poetry, but I find it difficult always to preserve the vague distinction which I had in my mind, for the most interesting and beautiful facts are so much the more poetry and that is their success . . . I see that if my facts were sufficiently vital and significant,— perhaps transmuted more into the substance of the human mind,—I should need but one book of poetry to contain them all." And as late as 1854 he makes the characteristic transcendental affirmation that "there is no such thing as pure *objective* observation." He continues: "The sum of what the writer of whatever class has to report is simply some human experience, whether he be poet or philosopher or man of science. The man of most science is the man most alive, whose life is the greatest event. Senses that take cognizance of outward things merely are of no avail . . . All that a man has to say or do that can possibly concern mankind, is in some shape or other to tell the story of his love,—to sing; and if he is fortunate and keeps alive, he will be forever in love." In passages like these our Bachelor of Nature is verging strongly toward a rhapsodic humanism.

As one surveys Thoreau's total deposit of words on paper, from his early journals and the *Week* through *Walden* to his posthumous travel books and the ten years of bookkeeping for all outdoors that constitutes the later journal, one cannot help being struck by an almost imperceptible shift of emphasis in practice from the poetic to the factual. It is as though Thoreau were passing within the compass of his own brief lifetime from a seventeenth-century view of a unified world of experience to a partial anticipation of the multiple universe characteristic of our own times. His earliest concern was for the depth and intensity of the life excited by his writing. He would attain to truth by the power of his pulses. "We cannot write well or truly but what we write with gusto. The body, the senses, must conspire with the mind. Expression is the act of the whole man, that our speech may be vascular . . . It is always essential that we love to do what we are doing, do it with a heart." Thoreau possessed by the vital urgency of his youth is not indifferent to the solidity and impact of his pages, but he is stimulated by the sheer ebullience of his energy into sportive pirouettings, puns, conceits, paradoxes, and verbal ingenuities. He is too effervescent to care greatly for the form of his writing. Any kind of framework will serve.

But as he becomes more sedate and factual the effervescence disappears, leaving only a negative scorn for the formal elements of composition. "It is surprising how much, from the habit of regarding writing as an accomplishment, is wasted on form. A very little information or wit is mixed up with a great deal of conventionalism in the style of expressing it, as with a sort of preponderating paste or vehicle. Some life is not simply expressed, but a long-winded speech is made, with an occasional attempt to put a little life in it." Instead of settling down to a "certain dryness" that he considered not incongruous with maturity of mind, Thoreau tried the dubious expedient of accumulating larger and larger stores of fresh factual impressions. Insensibly facts came to bulk larger than the use he could make of them. The sparkle of his earlier manner dimmed to sobriety.

The increase of information at the expense of wit was a natural consequence of the reaction from the artificial or mechanical sublimity of much early nineteenth-century romantic writing. With Emerson, Thoreau sought to poetize the commonplace, "the meal in the firkin, the milk in the pan." Homeliness stood high in his list of literary virtues. "There is a sort of homely truth and naturalness in some books," he wrote in 1841, "which is very rare to find, and yet looks quite cheap . . . The scholar rarely writes as well as the farmer talks. Homeliness is a great merit in a book; it is next to beauty and high art . . . I like better the surliness with which the woodchopper speaks of his woods, handling them as indifferently as his axe, than the mealy-mouthed enthusiasm of the lover of nature." It is possible to trace through the journals a gradual deterioration from homeliness to barrenness. At first Thoreau is captured by the challenge of making something out of a common theme. "I omit the unusual—the hurricanes and earthquakes—and describe the common. This has the greatest charm and is the true theme of poetry. You may have the extraordinary for your province if you will let me have the ordinary." Several years later the solid substance of out-of-door experiences is needed "as a ballast to thought and sentiment." Finally in 1858, still shying away from lofty subjects, Thoreau remarks: "It is a great art in the writer to improve from day to day just that soil and fertility which he has, to harvest that crop which his life yields, whatever it may be, not to be straining as if to reach apples or oranges when he yields only ground-nuts. He should be digging, not soaring." Thoreau had never been inclined to let his feet leave the ground. In the later years he became reconciled to digging.

The special luck of *Walden* among Thoreau's writings was to come neither too early nor too late, but at the happy moment when poetry and fact were in exquisite equilibrium. Some shadow of what was to come rests upon his recital of sundry measurements of the depth of the pond, the thickness of the ice, and the like, but on the whole it rests lightly. Meanwhile the "flame in the mind" illuminates with playful wit Thoreau's discussion of the economy of his sylvan retreat, and a passionate enjoyment of the freshness of life breathes from every page. The sentences are nervous and sensitive, stripped of all excess and flabbiness. Alcott paid his friend a deserved tribute in declaring: "Of Americans, Thoreau speaks and writes the strongest English . . . Nothing can be spared from his sentence; there is nothing superfluous or irrelevant, but all is compact, solid, and concrete, as Nature is."

11

Higher Laws

The keynote of literary aspiration for the period between 1830 and the Civil War was sounded by the elder William Ellery Channing, the Unitarian divine, when he replied to Charles J. Ingersoll's *Discourse Concerning the Influence of America on the Mind.* Speaking in Philadelphia before the American Philosophical Society in 1823, Ingersoll had argued that the mind of the new nation was practical and utilitarian, and that in consequence a true national literature should be expressed in works of utility rather than in *belles lettres.* Channing in his reply, published in 1830, was willing to agree that literature should not be divorced from life, but he could not tolerate the idea that either literature or life should be dominated by material interests. Instead he rèaffirmed the conviction previously voiced by Crèvecoeur that "the American is a new man, who acts upon new principles; he must therefore entertain new ideas, and form new opinions." But the novelty must attain the heights of a moral and spiritual revival. Here on an unpreempted continent mankind might be privileged to make a fresh beginning, sloughing off the old errors and inherited injustices of past centuries. Our literature should be founded on our hopes for the future, not on dark recollections of old-world defeats nor on a dull and sordid present.

"We want a reformation," exclaimed Channing. "We want a literature, in which genius will pay supreme, if not undivided homage, to truth and virtue . . . We should have no heart to encourage native literature, did we not hope that it would become instinct with a new spirit. We cannot admit the thought, that this country is to be only a repetition of the old world. We delight to believe that God, in the fulness of time, has brought a new continent to light, in order that the human mind should move here with a new freedom, should frame new social institutions, should explore new paths, and reap new harvests. We are accustomed to estimate nations by their creative energies, and we shall blush for our country, if, in circumstances so peculiar, original, and creative, it shall satisfy itself with a passive reception and mechanical reiteration of the thoughts of strangers."

This appeal for literary independence prepared the way for Emerson, who was but following out Channing's thought when he asked in *Nature* the fundamental question: "Why should not we also enjoy an original relation to the universe?" and proceeded in the *Essays* to develop his teaching of reliance on the godlike powers implicit in man's being. In an age of intellectual ferment newness and virtue often seemed synonymous, yet in actuality the two ideals that Channing hoped to realize in a national literature were not in all respects compatible. It is one thing for a writer to illustrate a lofty morality, and quite another for him to be informed by a new spirit. The principles of ethics are not a discovery of yesterday, but matter of venerable antiquity. Somewhere in the background of Channing's thought there seems to be lurking the characteristic American preconception that Europe holds a monopoly on sin. Our native genius would pay instinctive homage to truth and virtue if not contaminated from abroad. But Socrates and Saint Paul were not born in Boston.

The bifurcation, if not contradiction, inherent in Channing's argument did not lessen its attractiveness to American men of letters who immediately followed him. The notion of a fresh beginning which should involve at the same time a release from the baser side of human nature ran its course in the books of the three decades after 1830. The identification of newness and naturalness with truth and virtue is frequent in Thoreau, and traces of the same attitude may even be found in Henry James. Hawthorne was possibly the first to detect a potential opposition, as of Siamese twins, between the ideals of moral excellence and originality, while Melville may be said to have performed the fatal operation in his *Pierre* of cutting the two apart.

In the chapter of *Walden* called "Higher Laws" Thoreau is paying his homage to truth and virtue. The particular quality under discussion is purity of heart, which Thoreau associates with virginal freshness of the senses. "If the day and the night are such that you greet them with joy, and life emits a fragrance like flowers and sweet-scented herbs, is more elastic, more starry, more immortal,—that is your success." But the process by which Thoreau would attain this crowning bliss turns out to be the time-worn process of ascetic negation. He "would fain keep sober always; and there are infinite degrees of drunkenness . . . Of all ebriosity, who does not prefer to be intoxicated by the air he breathes?" Such a one may revel at a proper remove with Emily Dickinson, that "debauchee of dew," but he will be unprepared to sit down with Falstaff.

To a seeker after new ideas Thoreau's reflections on the satisfactions of a life of high moral purity must prove very disappointing. They would not be out of place in the mouth of a medieval anchorite, but they hardly advance the credit of a transcendental thinker. They are an almost perfect example of what Channing called the "mechanical reiteration of the thoughts of strangers," or of what are properly called ethical truisms. "Our whole life is startlingly moral. There is never an instant's truce between virtue and vice. Goodness is the only investment that never fails . . . We are conscious of an animal in us, which awakens in proportion as our higher nature slumbers . . . Chastity is the flowering of man; and what are called Genius, Heroism, Holiness, and the like, are but various fruits which succeed it . . . Nature is hard to be overcome, but she must be overcome." Some of these apothegms might worthily adorn *Poor Richard's Almanac*.

In the pages of *Walden* they represent a lapse into moral commonplace. Why go to the woods for such thoughts as these?

It may as well be conceded that Thoreau is somewhat deficient on the side of heartiness. This does not mean that he was gloomy. He could even be gay in society on rare occasions. There is a record of his singing his favorite song, "Here a sheer hulk lies poor Tom Bowling," with immense gusto and dancing a faun-like impromptu dance to the music of the piano in Daniel Ricketson's parlor, taking pains to tread now and then on the guileless Alcott's toes. But this outburst of high spirits appears almost unique. Either an acquired Puritanism or an ascetic strain derived from his oriental studies made Thoreau exaggerate the benefits of austerity and forget that to cultivate one's higher powers solely is not to improve but to mutilate human nature. It was an excessive prudery that made Thoreau reject Rabelais as coarse, and an excessive solemnity that induced him to qualify his admiration for Chaucer's *Prologue* by the remark that "it is esentially humorous as the loftiest genius never is," a remark which if taken literally would immediately relegate most of Thoreau's writing to the status of the second-rate. There was a vein of adamant in Thoreau's nature, and in some of his judgments he was inflexibly conventional.

But it is fair to say that he sometimes felt the burden of his derivative ethics and dropped them with relief. The chapter on "Higher Laws" opens significantly with Thoreau's confession that he would like to pursue a woodchuck and devour him raw. The flavor of wildness seemed to him a premonition of a sort of virtue that would never stale. A tangle of swamp where no man before him had penetrated was his substitute for Eden. "I love Nature partly *because* she is not man, but a retreat from him. None of his institutions control or pervade her. There a different kind of right prevails. In her midst I can be glad with an entire gladness. If this world were all man, I could not stretch myself, I should lose all hope. He is constraint, she is freedom to me. He makes me wish for another world. She makes me content with this." In preferring the "kind of right" that nature offers, Thoreau was becoming an American writer instinct with a new spirit.

It was not nature merely as the exterior world nor as the open air that he delighted in, but nature in its untouched and unsubdued wildness. He liked to keep out of sight of houses. In this respect he parted company with Wordsworth, who never wandered far from cottage and sheepfold. To Thoreau in his youth wildness was a thrilling and romantic experience, valued on the ground of its opposition to civilization. He hinted at its attractions in a famous passage in the *Week*:

"There is in my nature, methinks, a singular yearning toward all wildness . . . Gardening is civil and social, but it wants the vigor and freedom of the forest and the outlaw. There may be an excess of cultivation as well as of anything else, until civilization becomes pathetic . . . The young pines springing up in the corn-fields from year to year are to me a refreshing fact. We talk of civilizing the Indian, but that is not the name for his improvement. By the wary independence and aloofness of his dim forest life he preserves his intercourse with his native gods, and is admitted from time to time to a rare and peculiar society with Nature. He has glances of starry recognition to which our saloons are strangers. The steady illumination of his genius, dim only because distant, is like the faint but satisfying light of the stars compared with the dazzling but ineffectual and short-lived blaze of candles. The Society Islanders had their day-born gods, but they were not supposed to be 'of equal antiquity with the *atua fauau po,* or night-born gods!' "

From nature Thoreau next abstracted the quality of wildness and hypostatized it as an entity that might exist in the mind of man, in books, in actions. It was the matchless source of life and vigor, a reservoir of inexhaustible energy.

91

"In literature it is only the wild that attracts us." It is synonymous with genius. And finally, "in Wildness is the preservation of the World," the nourishment and tonic of mankind, as the still unsettled West was proving to be the salvation of the populated states. In the end nature was not sufficient to contain the degree of what might be called aboriginality that Thoreau desired. He was homesick for a wildness that could only be realized in imagination.

"We soon get through with Nature. She excites an expectation which she cannot satisfy. The merest child which has rambled into a copsewood dreams of a wilderness so wild and strange and inexhaustible as Nature can never show him."

.   .   .   .

"I long for wildness, a nature which I cannot put my foot through, woods where the wood thrush forever sings, where the hours are early morning ones, and there is dew on the grass, and the day is forever unproved, where I might have a fertile unknown for a soil about me. I would go after the cows, I would watch the flocks of Admetus there forever, only for my board and clothes. A New Hampshire everlasting and unfallen."

The dream of wildness thus came to stand to Thoreau as a symbol of the individuality, tang, and freshness of underivative things, and as such he held it precious. The exquisite unfolding of the leaves to fill out the pattern implicit in the seed, the unstudied grace of the bird balancing on the bough, the sureness of instinct in wild animals, these things were to him akin to the fulfillment of man's intellectual and spiritual powers. "We wish man on the higher plane to exhibit also the wildness or nature of that higher plane," wrote Emerson, and Thoreau entirely concurred. Beauty and integrity, magnanimity and a luminous mind should not be conscious contrivances, but organic flowerings of the primitive stock of human nature.

Toward the end of his life Thoreau ceased to look to nature as a means of romantic escape. He had come to see that wildness begins at home. "It is in vain to dream of a wildness distant from ourselves. There is none such . . . I shall never find in the wilds of Labrador any greater wildness than in some recess in Concord, *i.e.* than I import into it. A little more manhood or virtue will make the surface of the globe anywhere thrillingly novel and wild." So in his last phase Thoreau set to work to run down and corner the wildness that he could create in Concord. The enterprise was a part of his passionate pursuit of reality, which refused to stay put in either the inward or the outward world. Hundreds of pages of journal entries keeping minute record of the countryside in all its aspects, a million words of excerpts dealing with Indians, remained among his papers to testify to his unflagging zeal in the quest.

Francis Parkman is the only American writer comparable to Thoreau in his eagerness to capture in literature the most unique feature of American experience, the contact of civilized man with unbroken wilderness. His "History of the Forest," as he called his volumes on the struggle for the North American continent, is a magnificent achievement that by glimpses and flashes of indirection brings home to its readers a sense of how Europeans responding to a new environment were subtly changed into Americans, new men with new ideas. Thoreau attempted in a more personal way to portray the inwardness of this experience. For the last time in the world's history the freshness of an unviolated country, the wildness of the primitive forest, as American colonists had felt these things and as Thoreau could still in a measure recover them in Concord, were available to a writer who received them with deep reverence and attempted with vehement sincerity to transfer their inmost reality to his pages. Alcott has truly declared, "Of New England men, Thoreau came nearest to being indigenous."